Close Reading Companion

Mc
Graw
Hill
Education

Cover and Title Page: Nathan Love

www.mheonline.com/readingwonders

Copyright © McGraw-Hill Education

Send all inquiries to:
McGraw-Hill Education
Two Penn Plaza
New York, New York 10121

ISBN: 978-0-02-131025-8
MHID: 0-02-131025-4

Printed in the United States of America.

11 12 13 LMN 21 20 19 18

E

Eureka! I've Got It!

MEETING A NEED

REREAD *One Hen* 1

REREAD "Banks: Their Business and Yours" 4

INTEGRATE POETRY 7

TRIAL AND ERROR

REREAD *Second Day, First Impressions* 8

REREAD "Lost in the Museum Wings" 11

INTEGRATE PHOTOGRAPH 14

SEEING FOR YOURSELF

REREAD *Camping with the President* 15

REREAD "A Walk with Teddy" 18

INTEGRATE PHOTOGRAPH 21

INVENTIONS

REREAD *The Boy Who Invented TV* 22

REREAD "Time To Invent" 25

INTEGRATE FINE ART 28

TIME FOR KIDS

REREAD *The Future of Transportation* 29

REREAD "Getting From Here to There" 31

INTEGRATE SONG 33

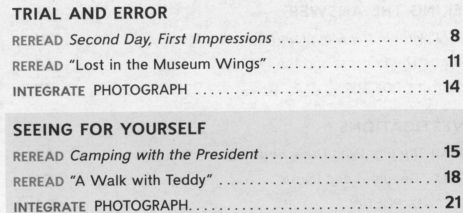

(t) Paul Rapson/Science Source, Inc; (b) Michael Dunning/Photographer's Choice/Getty Images

TAKING THE NEXT STEP

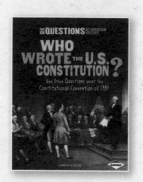

REACHING A COMPROMISE

REREAD *Who Wrote the U.S. Constitution?* 34

REREAD "Parchment and Ink" 37

INTEGRATE PHOTOGRAPH 40

SEEKING THE ANSWER

REREAD *Where the Mountain Meets the Moon* 41

REREAD "The Princess and the Pea" 44

INTEGRATE POETRY 47

INVESTIGATIONS

REREAD *The Boy Who Drew Birds* 48

REREAD "Daedalus and Icarus" 51

INTEGRATE POETRY 54

A PLAN OF ACTION

REREAD *Blancaflor* 55

REREAD "From Tale to Table" 58

INTEGRATE FINE ART 61

MAKING IT HAPPEN

REREAD "Stage Fright" 62

REREAD "Foul Shot" 64

INTEGRATE PHOTOGRAPH 66

Getting From Here to There

CULTURAL EXCHANGE

REREAD *They Don't Mean It!* **67**

REREAD "Where Did That Come From?" **70**

INTEGRATE SONG **73**

BEING RESOURCEFUL

REREAD *Weslandia.* **74**

REREAD "Plants with a Purpose" **77**

INTEGRATE POETRY **80**

PATTERNS

REREAD *The Story of Snow* **81**

REREAD "Fibonacci's Amazing Find" **84**

INTEGRATE FINE ART **87**

TEAMWORK

REREAD *Winter's Tail* **88**

REREAD "Helping Hands" **91**

INTEGRATE FINE ART **94**

TIME FOR KIDS

REREAD *Machu Picchu: Ancient City.* **95**

REREAD "Dig This Technology!" **97**

INTEGRATE PHOTOGRAPH **99**

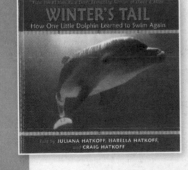

Yago Veith/Flickr/Getty Images; Turtle Pond Productions; TANAWAT LIKITKERERAT/National Geographic My Shot/National Geographic Stock

IT'S UP TO YOU

SHARING STORIES

REREAD *Davy Crockett Saves the World* **100**

REREAD "How Grandmother Spider Stole the Sun" **103**

INTEGRATE SONG **106**

DISCOVERIES

REREAD *A Window into History: The Mystery of the
Cellar Window* **107**

REREAD "A Second Chance For Chip: The Case of the
Curious Canine" **110**

INTEGRATE POETRY **113**

TAKE ACTION

REREAD *Rosa* **114**

REREAD "Our Voices, Our Votes" **117**

INTEGRATE PHOTOGRAPH **120**

CONSIDER OUR RESOURCES

REREAD *One Well* **121**

REREAD "The Dirt on Dirt" **124**

INTEGRATE FINE ART **127**

EXPRESS YOURSELF

REREAD "Words Free as Confetti" **128**

REREAD "A Story of How a Wall Stands" **130**

INTEGRATE FINE ART **132**

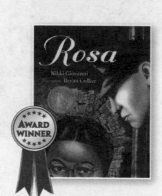

AWARD WINNER

AWARD WINNER

Brad Wilson/Stone/Getty Images

What's Next?

NEW PERSPECTIVES

REREAD *Ida B...and Her Plans to Maximize Fun, Avoid Disaster, and (Possibly) Save the World* 133

REREAD "A Dusty Ride" 136

INTEGRATE FINE ART 139

BETTER TOGETHER

REREAD *Bud, Not Buddy* 140

REREAD "Musical Impressions of the Great Depression" 143

INTEGRATE PHOTOGRAPH 146

OUR CHANGING EARTH

REREAD *Global Warming* 147

REREAD "When Volcanoes Erupt" 150

INTEGRATE POETRY 153

NOW WE KNOW

REREAD *When Is a Planet Not a Planet?* 154

REREAD "New Moon" 157

INTEGRATE FINE ART 160

TIME FOR KIDS

REREAD *The Case of the Missing Bees* 161

REREAD "Busy, Beneficial Bees" 163

INTEGRATE POETRY 165

Linked In

JOINING FORCES

REREAD *The Unbreakable Code*. 166

REREAD "Allies in Action" 169

INTEGRATE FINE ART 172

GETTING ALONG

REREAD *The Friend Who Changed My Life*. 173

REREAD "Choose Your Strategy: A Guide to Getting Along" . . 176

INTEGRATE FABLE 179

ADAPTATIONS

REREAD *Survival at 40 Below*. 180

REREAD "Why the Evergreen Trees Never Lose Their Leaves" 183

INTEGRATE PHOTOGRAPH 186

MAKING A DIFFERENCE

REREAD *Planting the Trees of Kenya* 187

REREAD "The Park Project". 190

INTEGRATE FINE ART 193

OUT IN THE WORLD

REREAD "You are My Music (Tú eres mi música)" 194

REREAD "A Time to Talk" 196

INTEGRATE POETRY 198

(t to b) Image Source/Getty Images; Martin Ruegner/Photographer's Choice RF/Getty Images

One Hen

Literature Anthology:
pages 10–23

? **How does the author help you understand the future Kojo dreams about?**

COLLABORATE

Talk About It Reread the last five paragraphs on page 12. Turn to your partner and talk about what Kojo's plans are.

Cite Text Evidence What words and phrases tell about Kojo's plan for the future? Write text evidence and tell why it's important to the story.

Text Evidence	Why It's Important

Write The author describes Kojo's dreams because _____

_____

CLOSE READING **Tip of the Week**

When I **reread**, I can think about how the author uses words and phrases. I look for text evidence to answer questions.

José

Jupiterimages/Getty Images

? **How does the author organize the events in the story to help you understand how one hen impacts Kojo's life?**

COLLABORATE

Talk About It Reread page 18. Turn to your partner and describe what is happening in Kojo's life.

Cite Text Evidence How is each event in Kojo's life connected to the one before it? Write text evidence.

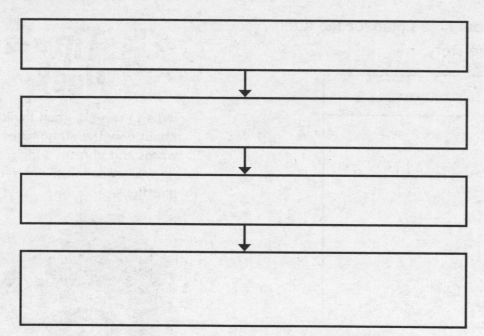

Write The author helps me understand how one hen impacts Kojo's life by _____

_____

_____

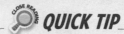
QUICK TIP

I can use these sentence frames when we talk about how the events in the story are organized.

I notice that the author . . .

I see that each event is . . .

? **How do you know that Kojo's dream will continue to come true?**

 **QUICK TIP**

I can think about how the author uses causes and effects to help me understand what a character does and why.

COLLABORATE

Talk About It Reread page 21. Talk with a partner about why Kojo gives Adika a loan.

Cite Text Evidence What clue tells you that Kojo is always thinking about the future? Use the chart to record text evidence.

Cause	Effect

Write I know that Kojo's dream will continue because the author _____

_____

_____

Your Turn

How does the author help you understand how Kojo changes and how he changes the lives of so many people? Use these sentence frames to organize your text evidence.

Katie Smith Milway begins and ends the story . . .

She uses cause and effect to . . .

This helps me understand . . .

Go Digital!
Write your response online.

Banks: Their Business and Yours

What is a Bank?

1 A bank is a business. But instead of making or selling things like computers, clothing, or cars, a bank provides services that involve money. Two basic services that a bank provides are savings accounts and loans.

2 Savings accounts help people save money for things they might need in the future, such as paying for college. Putting money in a savings account is like saving money in a piggy bank. But when you put money in a savings account, the bank pays you extra money, called interest. The interest is a reward for keeping your money in the bank. It also helps your savings grow.

Reread and use the prompts to take notes in the text.

Circle the sentence that the author uses to help you understand why a bank is a business. Write how a bank is a business here.

_____

_____

Talk with your partner about why the author uses the example of a piggy bank to explain what banks do. Explain your answer and underline text evidence in paragraph 2.

How Do Banks Help Us?

1 Think about what life would be like without banks. You might still find a safe place to keep your money. But your money wouldn't earn interest, and your savings wouldn't grow as quickly.

2 Without banks, you might still be able to get a loan. But it would be much harder to find one. Suppose you wanted a loan to buy a home or start a business. You would have to find a person or business willing to give you the money. This process would result in many fewer loans, and people would have a harder time meeting their needs and building businesses.

3 Thanks to banks, people have a place to go when they need to borrow money. You can see the results all around you. No matter where you live, banks are an important part of the community. They have helped many people buy homes, start businesses, and get a college education. They have helped people meet their needs and change their lives.

Reread paragraph 1. Circle two ways banks help us.

Then reread paragraph 2. Make marks in the margin beside reasons why people need loans.

COLLABORATE

Reread paragraph 3. Underline three examples that tell how a bank can affect a community. Talk with a partner about how the author feels about banks. Write text evidence here:

_____

_____

_____

? **How does the author organize the text to help you understand how banks help people?**

Talk About It Reread the excerpt on page 5. Talk with a partner about how the first and second paragraphs are different from the third paragraph.

Cite Text Evidence What clues help you understand how things would be different without banks? Write text evidence in the chart.

Text Evidence	What I Understand

Write The author helps me understand about banks by _____

_____

_____

QUICK TIP

When I **reread**, I can think about how the text is organized to help me understand about banks.

? How is the way the poet uses cause and effect in "Try Again" similar to the way the authors organize *One Hen* and "Banks: Their Business and Yours"?

COLLABORATE

Talk About It Read the poem. Talk with a partner about what the poet wants you to know and how the poem is organized.

Cite Text Evidence Reread the poem. Circle the phrase the poet repeats. Underline words and phrases that tell what would happen if you follow the poet's advice. This is the effect. Draw a box around the cause. Think about how the authors use cause and effect in the selections you read this week.

Write The poet's use of cause and effect is similar to _____

_____

_____

_____

Andrew Unangst/Getty Images

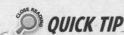
QUICK TIP

I see cause and effect in this poem. This will help me compare it to the selections I read this week.

Try Again

If you find your task is hard,
  Try again;
Time will bring you your reward,
  Try again.
All that other folks can do,
With your patience should not you?
Only keep this rule in view—
  Try again.

— Anonymous

Second Day, First Impressions

? How does the author use words and phrases to help you understand how Luisa feels at the beginning of the story?

Literature Anthology: pages 30–39

Talk About It Reread the first paragraph on page 31. Turn to your partner and talk about how Luisa feels when she first arrives at the park.

Cite Text Evidence What idioms does the author use to show how Luisa is feeling? Write text evidence in the chart.

Text Evidence	How Luisa Feels

Write The author's use of idioms helps me to understand _____

_____

CLOSE READING

Tip of the Week

When I **reread**, I can think about how the author uses words and phrases. I look for text evidence to answer questions.

Maddy

Lokibaho/Getty Images

How do you know that Luisa is changing?

COLLABORATE

Talk About It Reread page 35. Turn to your partner and discuss how Luisa feels after being wrong.

Cite Text Evidence What words and phrases show how Luisa is changing? Write text evidence in the chart below.

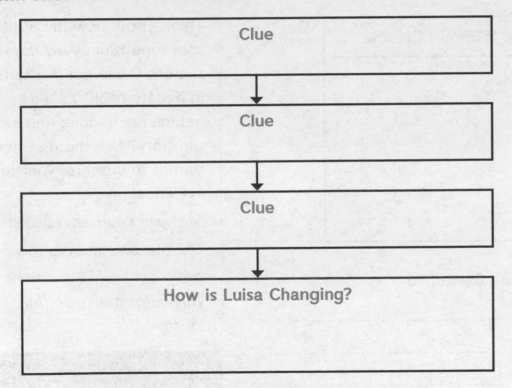

```
┌─────────────────────────────────────────┐
│                  Clue                     │
└─────────────────────────────────────────┘
                    ↓
┌─────────────────────────────────────────┐
│                  Clue                     │
└─────────────────────────────────────────┘
                    ↓
┌─────────────────────────────────────────┐
│                  Clue                     │
└─────────────────────────────────────────┘
                    ↓
┌─────────────────────────────────────────┐
│          How is Luisa Changing?           │
│                                           │
└─────────────────────────────────────────┘
```

Write I know that Luisa is changing because the author _____

_____

_____

 **QUICK TIP**

I can use these sentence frames when we talk about how Luisa feels.

After Luisa guesses wrong, she . . .

Her thoughts help me understand that . . .

? **How does the author use dialogue to show how things have changed for Luisa?**

COLLABORATE

Talk About It Reread page 39. Talk with a partner about what Luisa's team members say to her at the end of the race.

Cite Text Evidence What do the team members and Luisa say to each other? Write text evidence.

Text Evidence	How It Shows Change

Write I know that things for Luisa changed because the author _____

_____

_____

QUICK TIP
When I **reread**, I can use what the characters say to help me understand how they change.

Your Turn

Think about how the author uses repetition. Why does she use the idiom "butterflies in her stomach" at the beginning, middle, and end of the story? Use these sentence frames to organize your text evidence.

Michelle Knudsen repeats . . .

The reason she does this is to . . .

This helps me know that Luisa . . .

Go Digital!
Write your response online.

Lost in the Museum Wings

1.   "In here? That's odd," Mrs. Roberts turned to look too, but all she saw was a flood of visitors pouring out of the hall.

2.   Then she noticed the back of a boy's head moving away from the group and immediately recognized it—James! When she looked back, the class was already making their way through the Meteor Maze. She'd have to act fast to get her son and catch up to the class. She gathered the three and said, "Come with me. I've got to get James. Now stay together."

3.   Together they hurried down the hall and caught up with James as he was rounding the corner into the Coral Corridor.

4.   "James, you can't just wander off when you know we must all stay together as a group," Mrs. Roberts chided.

5.   "Sorry—I wanted to get a look at those butterflies," James explained.

Reread and use the prompts to take notes in the text.

In paragraph 1, circle the phrase that helps you visualize how many people are at the museum.

Then underline clues in paragraph 2 that show what Mrs. Roberts's problem is. Write the three things she has to do here:

1. _____

2. _____

3. _____

COLLABORATE

Reread the rest of the excerpt. Talk with your partner about why James wandered off. Draw a box around the text evidence that supports your discussion.

1   They hurried away, but when they reached the next hall, a silence welcomed them. "This is way too quiet for our class. Do you think they've already left?" Emi worried.

2   The group passed displays filled with jewels, robes, and headdresses, but there was no sign of their class. James stopped suddenly. "Wait! Maybe it's not monarchs as in kings," he said.

3   "What other options are there?" Ian asked.

4   "Remember the butterflies?" James asked. "I bet we're supposed to see monarch *butterflies*!"

5   "Well, we won't have much time to find them if we have to hurry back to the guard," Mrs. Roberts said, checking her watch anxiously.

6   Kaitlin pointed to a wall. "Look—a map! Maybe we can find another way to the exhibit without having to go back."

7   Ian quickly deciphered it. "Here's an exhibit called Magnificent Monarchs and Stunning Swallowtails—it's just down those stairs!"

8   They quickly descended the stairs. There, they could see an exhibit, but it was enclosed in glass and had a special entrance.

Reread paragraphs 1–2. Circle words and phrases that the author uses to create suspense.

Reread paragraphs 3–5. Make marks in the margin beside clues that show how Mrs. Roberts and the students feel.

COLLABORATE

Reread paragraphs 6 and 7. Talk with a partner about what Kaitlyn and Ian's ideas are. Underline text evidence to support your discussion.

How does the author show you how the kids solved problems? Use text evidence and write your answer here:

_____

_____

_____

? How does the author use dialogue to create suspense?

Talk About It Reread the excerpt on page 12. Talk with a partner about how you know how the characters feel.

Cite Text Evidence What do the characters say that shows how they are feeling? Write text evidence in the chart.

What Characters Say	How They Feel

Write The author creates suspense by using dialogue to _____

_____

_____

How are the workers in the photograph like Luisa and her teammates in *Second Day, First Impressions* **and the group of students in "Lost in the Museum Wings"?**

COLLABORATE

Talk About It Look at the photograph and read the caption. Talk with a partner about what you see. Choose two or three people in the photo and discuss what they are doing.

Cite Text Evidence In the photograph, circle groups of people who are working together. How do you know that their job is a big one? Underline clues in the caption.

Write The workers in the photograph and characters in the stories are alike because _____

_____

_____

_____

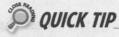

QUICK TIP

In the photograph, I see many people working together. This will help me compare it to the selections I read this week.

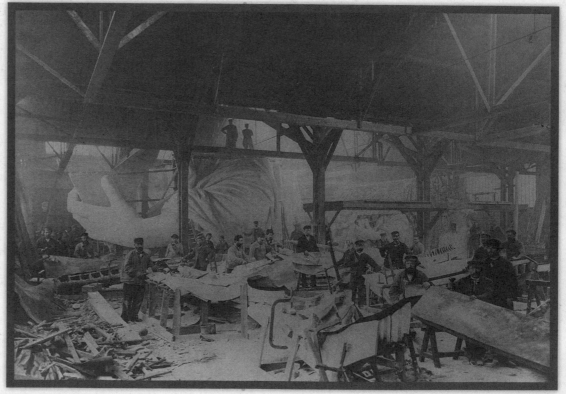

Library of Congress Prints and Photographs Division [LC-USZ62-20113]

This photograph was taken in 1882 in a warehouse in Paris, France. It is called, "Constructing the Statue of Liberty." Can you see her left hand in the photo?

Camping with the President

? How does the author help you visualize what President Roosevelt sees and hears at Yosemite?

COLLABORATE

Talk About It Reread pages 52–53. Turn to a partner and discuss how the author describes what President Roosevelt experiences.

Cite Text Evidence What words and phrases help you picture in your mind what President Roosevelt sees and hears? Write text evidence in the chart.

Text Evidence	What I Visualize

Write The author helps me visualize what Roosevelt sees and hears by _____

_____

_____

Literature Anthology: pages 46–61

CLOSE READING **Tip** of the **Week**

When I **reread**, I use the author's words to help me visualize what the character sees and feels.

Sofia

KidStock/Blend Images/Getty Images

? **How does the author help you understand why President Roosevelt decides to help John Muir?**

COLLABORATE

Talk About It Reread page 55. Turn to your partner and discuss how President Roosevelt reacts to what John Muir tells him.

Cite Text Evidence How does the author help you see how Roosevelt feels about the sequoia trees being cut down? Write text evidence in the chart.

Text Evidence	What He Plans To Do

Write I understand why Roosevelt helps Muir because the author _____

_____

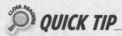I can use these sentence frames when we talk about what Roosevelt is thinking.

The author says that Roosevelt...

This helps me understand why he wants to...

? How does the author's use of dialogue help you visualize how President Roosevelt is affected by his night in the forest?

QUICK TIP
I can use dialogue to help me understand how the character feels.

COLLABORATE

Talk About It Reread page 58. Turn to a partner and talk about what President Roosevelt said.

Cite Text Evidence What does President Roosevelt say that shows how he feels? Write text evidence in the web.

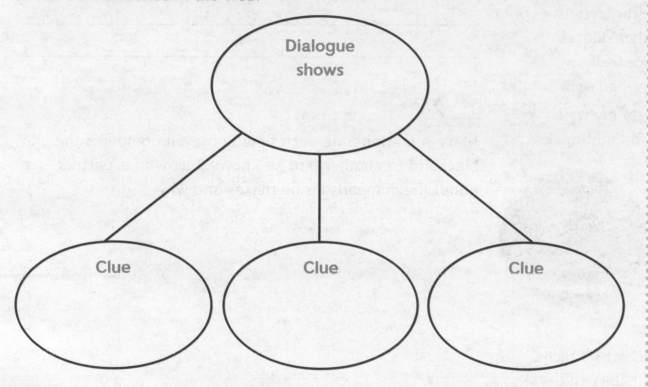

Dialogue shows

Clue

Clue

Clue

Write The author uses dialogue to help me understand that Roosevelt feels _____

_____

_____

Your Turn

Think about what President Roosevelt said and did while at Yosemite. How does the author show how Roosevelt changes because of his experience? Use these sentence frames to organize your text evidence.

The author tells about Roosevelt's trip by...

The dialogue and illustrations help me to...

This helps me understand that Roosevelt...

Go Digital!
Write your response online.

A Walk with Teddy

1   "We left London on the morning of June 9... Getting off the train at Basingstoke, we drove to the pretty, smiling valley of the Itchen. Here we tramped for three or four hours, then again drove, this time to the edge of the New Forest, where we first took tea at an inn, and then tramped through the forest to an inn on its other side, at Brockenhurst. At the conclusion of our walk my companion made a list of the birds we had seen...

2   The bird that most impressed me on my walk was the blackbird. I had already heard nightingales in abundance near Lake Como... but I had never heard either the blackbird, the song thrush, or the blackcap warbler; and while I knew that all three were good singers, I did not know what really beautiful singers they were. Blackbirds were very abundant, and they played a prominent part in the chorus which we heard throughout the day... In its habits and manners the blackbird strikingly resembles our American robin...

Reread and use the prompts to take notes in the text.

Reread paragraphs 1 and 2. Underline words and phrases that show what Theodore Roosevelt learned about blackbirds.

Circle one sentence that tells Roosevelt's opinion of blackbirds. Write it here:

_____

_____

COLLABORATE

Make a mark beside each time Roosevelt compares the blackbird to another bird he knows. Talk with a partner about the comparisons he makes and why.

Andrew Howe/Photodisc/Getty Images

A Man of Action

1. Roosevelt realized that seeing and hearing these birds in the wild gave him more information than any book. He could see the birds in action. He could hear their calls to each other. His experience revealed much about the birds of the country.

2. Roosevelt continued to travel throughout his life. He took every opportunity to study animals in the wild. But his travels also showed him that habitats needed to be protected. In his years as president, Roosevelt worked to preserve land. He established 150 national forests, 4 national parks, and 51 bird reservations. These sites continue to protect the nation's wildlife.

Elaine Mayes/Digital Vision/Getty Images

Reread paragraph 1. Circle all the ways that Roosevelt gained information about birds. Draw a box around what his experience taught him.

COLLABORATE

Reread paragraph 2. Look at the photograph and the caption. Underline the words that help you see how Roosevelt took action.

Talk with a partner about why "A Man of Action" is a good title for this section. Use your annotations and the photograph to support your response.

_____

_____

Roosevelt declared Crater Lake a national park. This lake is the deepest lake in the United States. It has a depth of 1,943 feet.

? **How do the excerpts, photograph, and caption help you see how Roosevelt's trip to England had a lasting impact on him?**

COLLABORATE

Talk About It Reread the excerpt on page 19 and look at the photograph. Talk about the things Roosevelt did after his trip to England.

Cite Text Evidence What are some of the things Roosevelt did? Use the web to record text evidence.

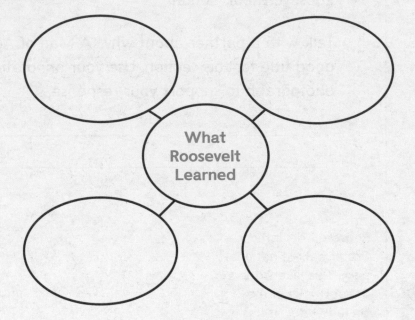

What
Roosevelt
Learned

Write I know Roosevelt's trip had an impact on his life because _____

_____

_____

QUICK TIP

When I **reread**, I can analyze the author's examples to help me understand an autobiography.

? How do the photographer and the authors of *Camping with the President* and "A Walk with Teddy" help you experience nature and change the way you think about it?

COLLABORATE

Talk About It Look at the photograph and read the caption. Talk with a partner about how it makes you feel and why.

Cite Text Evidence Underline the cause and effect of the "Bald Eagle Protection Act" noted in the caption. Circle three details in the photo that show how powerful and strong this bald eagle is. Think about how the authors use words and phrases to paint pictures of nature in the selections you read this week.

Write The photographer and authors help me

experience nature by _____

_____

_____

_____

_____

Alan and Sandy Carey/Getty Images

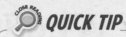
QUICK TIP

I can use details in the photograph to help me experience nature. This will help me compare text to art.

In 1940, the "Bald Eagle Protection Act" was passed to prevent bald eagles from going extinct. In 2007, the bird was no longer threatened because its population had greatly recovered.

The Boy Who Invented TV

Literature Anthology:
pages 68–83

How does the author help you visualize what Philo was like as a young boy?

COLLABORATE

Talk About It Reread page 71. Turn to your partner and talk about what Philo enjoyed doing as a child.

Cite Text Evidence What words and phrases help you understand what Philo was like as a boy? Write text evidence in the web.

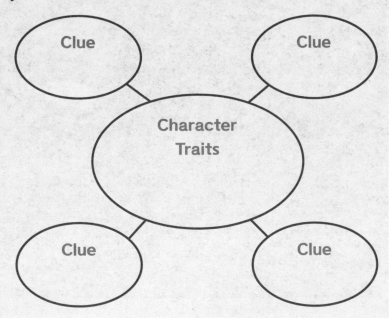

Clue

Clue

Character Traits

Clue

Clue

Tip of the Week

When I **reread**, I can use details to help me visualize what the character is like.

Evan

Write The author helps me visualize what Philo was like as a boy by _____

_____

_____

? **How do you know how Philo feels about science?**

COLLABORATE

Talk About It Reread the first four paragraphs on page 78. Turn to your partner and talk about what Philo is doing.

Cite Text Evidence What clues tell you how Philo feels about science? Write text evidence here.

How Philo usually acts	How Philo talks about science	Inferences

Write I know how Philo feels about science because the author _____

_____

_____

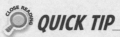

? **How does the author help you understand how Philo feels about his dream of inventing television?**

COLLABORATE

Talk About It Reread the last two paragraphs on page 80. Talk with a partner about Philo's vision for television.

Cite Text Evidence What words and phrases show what Philo is envisioning for the future of television? Write text evidence in the chart.

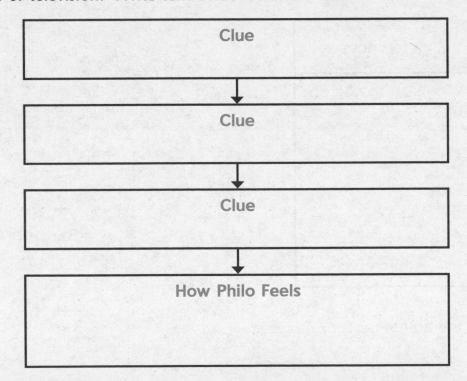

Clue

↓

Clue

↓

Clue

↓

How Philo Feels

Write The author helps me understand Philo's dream by _____

_____

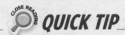
QUICK TIP

As I reread, I can use the author's words and phrases to help me understand how a character feels.

Your Turn

How does the author help you understand how passionate Philo was about his dream of inventing television? Use these sentence frames to organize your text evidence.

Kathleen Krull begins the story of Philo by...

She focuses on his...

This helps me understand that Philo invented television to...

Go Digital!
Write your response online.

Time to Invent

Monday 8:00PM

1   That night, after much pleading from Lydia, her mom agreed to let her have another try. Not wanting to take any chances that she'd sleep through the alarm, she turned the volume on the alarm up—way up. It didn't seem like the most soothing way to wake up, but Lydia was pretty sure it would do the trick.

Tuesday 7:50AM

2   The next morning, a piercing beeping echoed through her room, jolting her awake. While Lydia fumbled with the off button on the alarm, her mother came running into the room with her hands over her ears. "What is that awful noise?" her mother cried. Lydia hit the alarm off.

3   "Well, at least I am up on time," she mumbled with embarrassment.

4   Her mother gave her an exasperated look. "And so is the whole neighborhood!"

5   Although Lydia made it to the bus on time that day, she knew her mother would never stand for that every morning. If she was going to convince her mom, she would have to think of a better way to get herself up.

Reread and use the prompts to take notes in the text.

Reread paragraphs 2–4. Underline phrases that help you visualize how Lydia woke up Tuesday morning. Circle clues in the illustration that give you more information. Write them here.

_____

_____

COLLABORATE

Reread paragraph 5. Talk with your partner about how you know that Lydia is going to keep trying. Make a mark in the margin beside the text evidence.

Tuesday 3:30PM

6 When Lydia got home from school that day, her mother asked Lydia to help her find her old cell phone. "I got a new one this afternoon. I want to give you my old one, but I can't find it anywhere." Her mother dialed her old number while Lydia searched the house. In the kitchen, she heard a muffled rattle coming from a drawer. Lydia opened the drawer, and there, shaking among the pens and pads of paper, was her mother's cell phone.

7 Suddenly, Lydia had a breakthrough. "Mom, I found it," she said, answering the phone. "And will you give me one more chance to wake myself up tomorrow?"

8 That afternoon, Lydia figured out how to set the phone alarm to vibrate. Then she went to the kitchen and looked through the recycling bin. She found a metal coffee can and matching lid, washed them out, and took them upstairs. She set the phone alarm to vibrate, put the phone in the coffee can, and covered it with the lid. She counted the seconds until the alarm went off: 3-2-1. Suddenly, the can rattled and shook as the phone vibrated against it.

Reread paragraphs 6 and 7. Underline clues that show that Lydia has a new idea. Write them here:

_____

_____

COLLABORATE

Reread paragraph 8. Talk with a partner about the steps Lydia takes. Write numbers in the margin beside the steps she takes to create her invention.

Circle the words that show time order.

? **Why is "Time to Invent" a good title for this story?**

Talk About It Reread the excerpt on page 26. With a partner, talk about how and why Lydia created her invention.

Cite Text Evidence What clues support the author's choice to use "Time to Invent" as the title of the story? Write text evidence in the chart.

Text Evidence	"Time to Invent"

Write "Time to Invent" is a good title for this story because _____

_____

_____

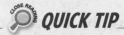
QUICK TIP

When I **reread**, I will find text evidence to help me understand the author's purpose.

? **How is the way the artist shows this moment in the Transcontinental Railroad's history similar to how the authors describe Philo's work in _The Boy Who Invented TV_ and Lydia's goal in "Time to Invent"?**

COLLABORATE

Talk About It With a partner, discuss what is going on in the painting. Read the caption. Talk about what you see and what the railroads connect.

Cite Text Evidence Look at the painting. Circle the focal point of the painting. Work with a partner to find three other points of interest in the painting. Make notes in the margin about why each one is interesting.

Write The artist and authors both show

_____

_____

_____

_____

_____

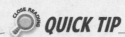

QUICK TIP

When I look at the painting, my eye is drawn to the center. What I see there helps me compare this painting to the selections I read this week.

GOLDEN SPIKE

Architect of the Capitol

Railroad workers celebrate the connection of two railroads in Promontory, Utah. It hangs in the Westward Expansion Hall of the U.S. Capitol Building in Washington, D.C.

The Future of Transportation

? How do you know how the author of "Autos Advance" feels about cars?

Talk About It Reread page 91. Turn to your partner and discuss how the author compares modern cars and public transportation.

Cite Text Evidence What words and phrases help you understand the author's point of view? Write text evidence to support his opinion.

Public Transportation	Cars

Write I know how the author feels about cars because he _____

_____

_____

Literature Anthology:
pages 90–93

CLOSE READING **Tip of the Week**

When I **reread**, I can use text evidence to understand the author's point of view.

Candice

Blend Images - JGI/Jamie Grill/Brand X Pictures/Getty Images

? How do text features help you understand how the author of "The Rail Way" feels about public transportation?

Talk About It Look at the text features on pages 92–93. Turn to your partner and talk about how they support the author's argument.

Cite Text Evidence What new and persuasive information did you learn by using the text features? Write evidence here.

Headings	Photographs	Captions

Write The author uses text features to _____

_____

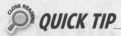

QUICK TIP
I can analyze text features to understand more about an author's point of view.

Your Turn

Think about how the authors present their positions on transportation technology. How do they support their arguments? Cite evidence from the text using these sentence frames.

In their arguments, each author...

This helps me understand that...

Go Digital!
Write your response online.

Getting From Here to There

[1]   Passengers are not the only ones moving along these days. Transportation technology is moving along, too. Cars and trains are changing at a rapid pace. These advances may offer more ways of getting around in the future.

The Ways People Commute

[2]   While transportation researchers may count train passengers or the number of cars passing a toll, a survey is another way experts collect data. A government survey analysis showed most people get to work by personal vehicle. Some people interpret this to mean it is the preferred way to travel. Improving public transportation could change that.

▨ Car, truck, or van	88%
▮ Bus	3%
▮ Walked	3%
▨ Worked from home	3%
▢ Railroad or subway	2%
▨ Other	1%

Source: U.S. Census Bureau, 2000 Summary File 3.

Chuck Eckert/Alamy

Reread and use the prompts to take notes in the text.

Reread paragraph 1. Underline the sentence that shows how the author feels about transportation technology. Draw a box around the sentence in paragraph 2 that transitions to the pie chart.

COLLABORATE

Look at the pie chart. Talk with a partner about what each part of the chart represents. How do you know which way is the most popular way people commute? Circle the clue.

Draw an arrow to the least popular way people commute.

? How does the author help you understand how data can support improvements in transportation?

Talk About It Reread the excerpt on page 31 and look at the pie chart. Talk with a partner about how the author's use of a chart helps get her point across.

Cite Text Evidence How does the pie chart help make technical information easier to understand? Write evidence in the web below.

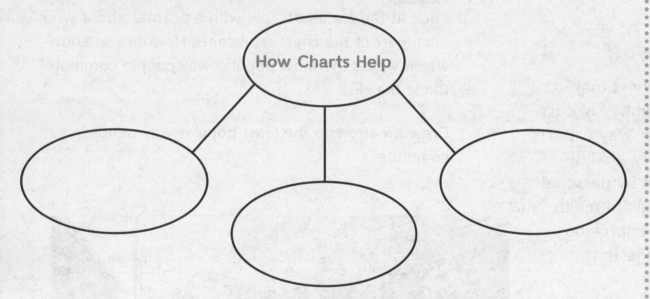

How Charts Help

Write The author's use of text features helps me understand _____

_____

_____

 **QUICK TIP**

When I **reread**, I can use text features to help me understand technical information.

? How is the songwriter's message about transportation similar to the opinions of the authors of "The Future of Transportation" and "Getting from Here to There"?

Talk About It Read the song lyrics. Talk with a partner about what the songwriter's message is. Discuss what it has in common with the selections you read this week about transportation.

Cite Text Evidence In the song lyrics, circle phrases that tell how the writer feels about train travel. Underline clues that show why the writer feels this way.

Write The songwriter's message is similar to what the authors think because _____

_____

_____

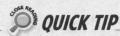

QUICK TIP

The lyrics help me understand how the songwriter feels. This helps me compare the song to the selections I read this week.

Down Yonder

Railroad train, railroad train,
   hurry some more;
Put a little steam on just like
   never before.
Hustle on, bustle on, I've got
   the blues,
Yearning for my Swanee
   shore.
Brother if you only knew, you'd
   want to hurry up, too.

— L. Wolfe Gilbert, 1921.

Who Wrote the U.S. Constitution?

? How does the sidebar give you more insight into the role James Madison played in the Virginia Plan?

COLLABORATE

Talk About It Reread page 103. Turn to your partner and talk about what the information in the sidebar tells you.

Cite Text Evidence What words and phrases in the sidebar tell you more about James Madison? Write text evidence and tell why it's important.

Text Evidence	Why It's Important

Write The author uses the sidebar to _____

_____

Literature Anthology:
pages 96–111

Tip of the **Week**

When I **reread**, I think about how the author uses text features to organize information. I look for text evidence to answer questions.

Oscar

Hola Images/Getty Images

? **How does the author build suspense in "The Great Compromise"?**

COLLABORATE

Talk About It Reread page 104. Turn to your partner and discuss how the author describes what happened on July 2, 1787.

Cite Text Evidence What words and phrases does the author use to create suspense? Write text evidence in the chart.

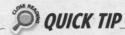
QUICK TIP

I can use these sentence frames when we talk about how the author builds suspense.

The author uses phrases to describe . . .

This creates suspense because . . .

Text Evidence	How It Builds Suspense

Write The author builds suspense by _____

_____

_____

? **How does the author help you understand how Benjamin Franklin's outlook changes?**

COLLABORATE

Talk About It Reread the last two paragraphs on page 110. Talk to a partner about what Franklin thought about the carving on Washington's chair.

Cite Text Evidence How does what Franklin thinks about the carving indicate that his outlook changed? Use text evidence to explain.

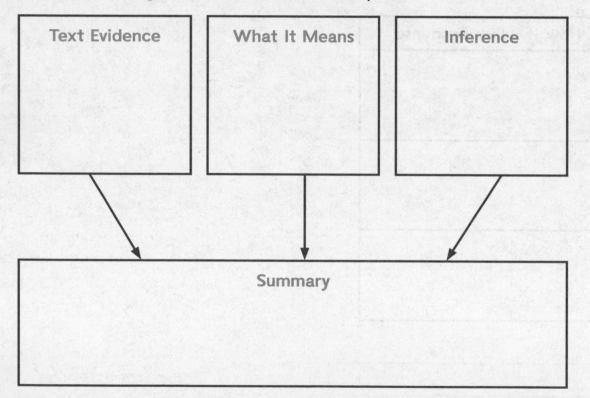

Text Evidence	What It Means	Inference

Summary

Write I know Benjamin Franklin's outlook has changed because _____

_____

QUICK TIP

When I reread, I can use the author's words and phrases to help me understand how things change.

Your Turn

How does the author help you understand that the decisions the delegates made affected not only them but all Americans? Use these sentence frames to organize your text evidence.

Candice Ransom uses text features to . . .

She creates suspense by . . .

This helps me see that the delegates . . .

Go Digital!
Write your response online.

Parchment and Ink

National Archives and Records Administration

1   The Declaration of Independence and the United States Constitution express our nation's most enduring ideas. However, both are also 200-year-old physical objects. Written in ink on parchment, they are fragile. Fire, water, sunlight, and air—these can damage documents. So it's amazing that we still can read the original Declaration and Constitution. It has taken the efforts of many people to preserve these treasures.

2   The Declaration was approved in July 1776. Soon afterward, Congress assigned someone to handwrite it in ink in clear letters. It was written with a quill pen, a pen made from the tip of a feather, on a sheet of parchment, a thin, strong material made from animal skin. This document was then signed by most members of Congress.

3   The Declaration was official and beautiful. It traveled with Congress from Philadelphia to Baltimore and back. At different times, it was housed in Pennsylvania and New Jersey. It was later moved to the nation's new capital in Washington, D.C. The document was moved a lot during the American Revolution in order to protect it.

Reread and use the prompts to take notes in the text.

Reread paragraph 1. Circle what the Declaration of Independence and the United States Constitution have in common. Draw a box around the four things that can damage the documents. Write them here:

1. _____

2. _____

3. _____

4. _____

COLLABORATE

Talk with your partner about how the author feels about these original documents. Underline clues in the excerpt that support your ideas.

In the Librarian's Care

[1]   The Constitution was not damaged as much as the Declaration of Independence. It traveled with the Declaration through 1814. Then the Constitution remained in the care of the State Department until 1921. That year, both documents were given to the Library of Congress.

[2]   The Librarian of Congress treasured them. He wanted people to be able to see these important documents but also wanted people to make sure they were protected. He decided to place the documents in what he called a "shrine" or sacred space, surrounded by marble. The documents were framed but protected from natural light by double panes of glass. A special coating was added to the glass to further exclude light. A guard was posted to watch over both documents.

Reread paragraph 2. Circle how the Librarian of Congress felt about the documents. Mark in the margin the steps the librarian took to protect the documents.

COLLABORATE

With a partner, look at the photograph and read the caption. Talk about how the documents are being preserved. What new information did you learn? Underline text evidence in the caption and circle clues in the photograph that support your discussion.

In 1951, the Declaration and the Constitution were sealed in cases filled with helium gas. Later, these cases were carefully opened. The documents were studied before being placed in new cases. Experts took samples of the ink to learn how to better protect it.

? Why did the author write "Parchment and Ink"?

Talk About It Reread the excerpts on pages 37 and 38. Talk with a partner about how the documents were treated and preserved.

Cite Text Evidence What does the author want you to know about the documents? Write text evidence in the chart.

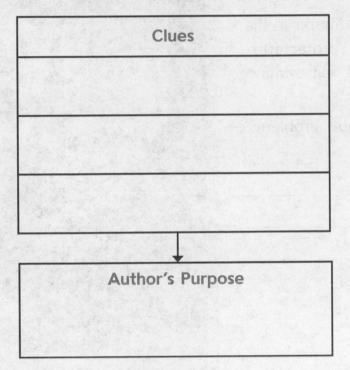

Clues

Author's Purpose

Write The author wrote "Parchment and Ink" to _____

_____

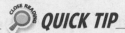

QUICK TIP

When I **reread**, I look for text evidence to figure out the author's purpose.

? How do the photographer and the authors of *Who Wrote the U.S. Constitution?* and "Parchment and Ink" help you understand how problems get solved?

COLLABORATE

Talk About It Look at the photograph and read the caption. Talk with a partner about how the bell is displayed and what has been done to keep it safe.

Cite Text Evidence With a partner, circle two historical landmarks in the photograph. Identify two ways that the Liberty Bell has been protected and write them in the margin. Reread the caption. Underline text evidence that tells one more.

Write The photographer and authors help me understand how problems

get solved by _____

_____

_____

_____

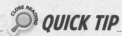

QUICK TIP

I see the Liberty Bell and how it is displayed. This will help me compare the photograph to the selections I read this week.

NPS Photo

The Liberty Bell is on display at the Liberty Bell Center in Philadelphia, PA. It cracked the first time it was rung when it arrived here. It was recast twice after that.

Where the Mountain Meets the Moon

Literature Anthology:
pages 118–131

? How does the author's use of figurative language help you understand how Minli feels?

Talk About It Reread the last five paragraphs on page 123. Turn to your partner and talk about Minli's feelings.

Cite Text Evidence What phrases does the author use to help you visualize how MInli feels? Record text evidence in the chart.

Tip of the Week

When I **reread**, I will think about how the author uses figurative language to help me visualize the characters' feelings. I look for text evidence to answer questions.

Figurative Language	Meaning

Kara

Write The author's use of figurative language helps me understand _____

_____

_____

Jodi Matthews/iStock/360/Getty Images

? **How does the author use foreshadowing to help you understand more about the lions' story?**

COLLABORATE

Talk About It Reread the last two paragraphs on page 127. Talk to a partner about how the author hints about events in the next part of the story.

Cite Text Evidence What phrases help you figure out what happens next? Write text evidence in the chart.

Text Evidence	What It Means

Write The author's use of foreshadowing helps me to understand _____

_____

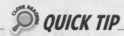
QUICK TIP

I can use these sentence frames when we talk about the author's use of foreshadowing.

The author uses foreshadowing to . . .

This helps me know that the lions . . .

? How does the male lion's "String of Destiny" story allow the author to share information with you that was not in the king's story?

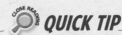

QUICK TIP

When I **reread**, I can think about how the author structures the story.

Talk About It Reread pages 128–129. Talk to a partner about how the "String of Destiny" story reveals information that was not in the king's story.

Cite Text Evidence How is the lion's story different from the king's story? How is it the same? Record text evidence in the diagram.

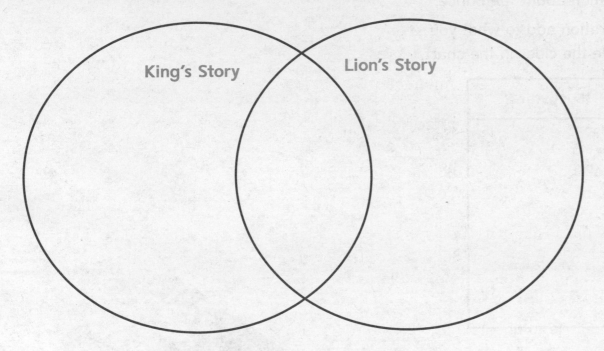

King's Story   Lion's Story

Write The author uses the male lion's story to share more information because

_____

_____

_____

Your Turn

How does Grace Lin show that the king and the male lion both give up something important to them? Use these sentence frames to organize your text evidence.

Grace Lin uses figurative language to . . .

She helps me understand . . .

This helps me see that the king and the male lion . . .

Go Digital!
Write your response online.

The Princess and the Pea

? How does the author use the illustration to help you identify the Prince's mood?

Talk About It Reread page 134. With a partner, analyze the illustration. Talk about clues that give you more information about the Prince.

Cite Text Evidence What clues in the illustration add to what you already read about the Prince's mood? Write the clues in the chart.

Text Evidence	Illustration

Write The author uses the illustration of the Prince to _____

_____

QUICK TIP

I can use illustrations to help me understand how a character feels.

? How does the author use sensory language to help you visualize the events of the fairy tale?

Talk About It Reread page 136. Talk with a partner about how the princess feels in the morning after sleeping all night on a pea.

Cite Text Evidence How does the author help you visualize how the princess feels? Write text evidence and tell what you visualize.

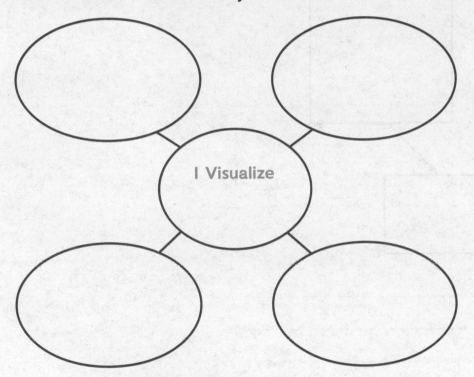

I Visualize

Write The author uses sensory language to help me visualize _____

_____

_____

 **QUICK TIP**

When I reread, I can use sensory language to help me visualize the events in a fairy tale.

How does the author use humor to set the tone of the fairy tale?

COLLABORATE

Talk About It Reread page 137. Turn to a partner and talk about how the author ends the fairy tale.

Cite Text Evidence What words and phrases add humor? Write text evidence in the chart and explain how the author adds humor to the fairy tale.

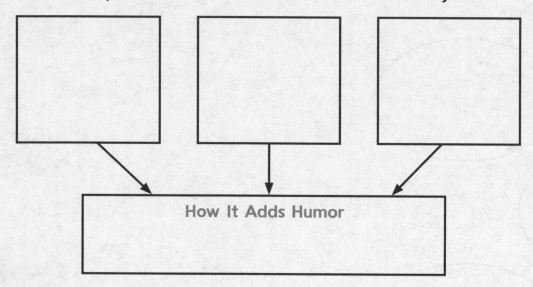

How It Adds Humor

Write The author uses humor in the fairy tale to _____

_____

_____

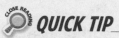 **QUICK TIP**

I can use these sentence frames when we talk about the author's use of humor.

The author uses words and phrases that are funny to . . .

This helps me feel . . .

Integrate

? How is the way the poet helps you visualize how answers are found similar to the way the authors use descriptive language in *Where the Mountain Meets the Moon* and "The Princess and the Pea"?

Talk About It With a partner, read the poem. Talk about how the poet shows how information is learned.

Cite Text Evidence Circle clues in the poem that help you visualize what a hippopotamus is like. Underline words and phrases that tell what the word *hippopotamus* means.

Write I can visualize how answers are found because _____

_____

_____

_____

_____

Ingram Publishing/SuperStock

 **QUICK TIP**

I see words and phrases in the poem that help me visualize. This will help me compare the poem with the texts.

The Hippopotamus

"OH, say, what is this fearful,
wild Incorrigible cuss?"
"This *creature* (don't say 'cuss,' my child;
'Tis slang) — this creature fierce is styled
The Hippopotamus.
His curious name derives its source
From two Greek words: *hippos* — a horse,
Potamos — river. See?
The river's plain enough, of course;
But why they called *that* thing a *horse*,
That's what is Greek to me."

—Oliver Herford

The Boy Who Drew Birds

Literature Anthology:
pages 138–149

? How does the illustration help you understand how John James conducted research on birds?

COLLABORATE

Talk About It Look at pages 140 and 141. Turn to your partner and discuss what the illustration tells you about John James and his methods.

Cite Text Evidence What clues in the illustrations show how John James researched birds? Write the clues in the chart.

CLOSE READING **Tip** of the **Week**

Illustration	What I Learned

When I **reread**, I can think about how the illustrations help me understand the text. I look for text evidence to answer questions.

Darius

Write The illustration helps me understand _____

_____

_____

? **Why does the author describe what other scientists believed about birds?**

Talk About It Reread page 143. Turn to your partner and talk about what John James thought about the writings of Aristotle and modern day scientists.

Cite Text Evidence Why does the author want you to know what John James thought of other scientists' work regarding birds? Write text evidence.

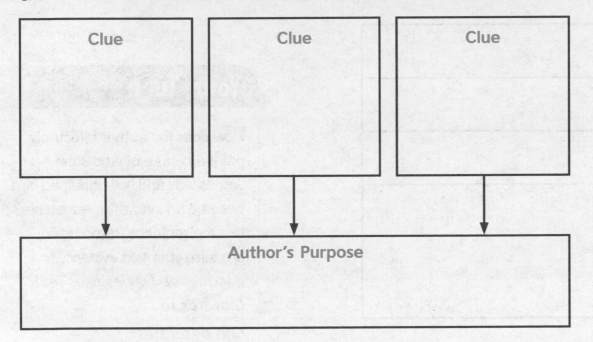

Clue	Clue	Clue

Author's Purpose

Write The author describes what other scientists thought to _____

_____

_____

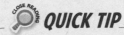 **QUICK TIP**

I can use these sentence frames when we talk about the author's purpose.

The author says that other scientists believed...

This helps me understand that John James...

? How does the author use descriptive language to help you understand how John James feels when the birds return?

COLLABORATE

Talk About It Reread paragraph 6 on page 147. Turn to a partner and talk about how the author describes the birds' behavior.

Cite Text Evidence What words and phrases help you understand the importance of the birds' return? Write evidence in the chart.

Detail
Detail
Detail
How John James Feels

Write The author's descriptive language helps me understand that John feels

_____

_____

_____

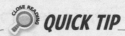
QUICK TIP

I can use descriptive details about events in John James' biography to help me understand how he feels.

Your Turn

How does the author effectively paint a picture of who John James was and how it helped him become an innovative researcher? Use the sentence frames to organize your text evidence.

Jacqueline Davies uses text features to...

She describes...

This helps me understand that John James...

Go Digital!
Write your response online.

Daedalus and Icarus

? How does the author's use of dialogue tell you about the kind of person Daedalus is?

Talk About It Reread page 153. Turn to a partner and talk about how Daedalus reacts to what Minos says.

Cite Text Evidence What does Daedalus say that helps you understand how he feels? Write evidence in the chart.

Clues

↓

How Daedalus Feels

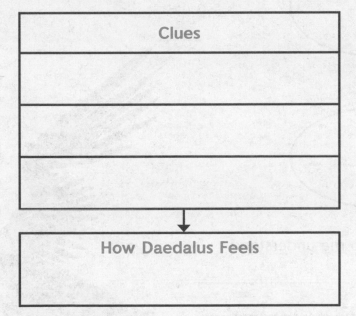

Write The author helps me understand how Daedalus feels by _____

_____

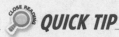

? **What do Daedalus's actions on the day of the flight tell you about his character?**

Talk About It Reread page 154. Turn to a partner and talk about what Daedalus does before the flight and when he sees where Icarus is going.

Cite Text Evidence What words and phrases show what Daedalus is like? Write text evidence in the web.

 QUICK TIP

I can use these sentence frames when we talk about Daedalus's character.

The author describes what Daedalus says and does by...

This helps me understand...

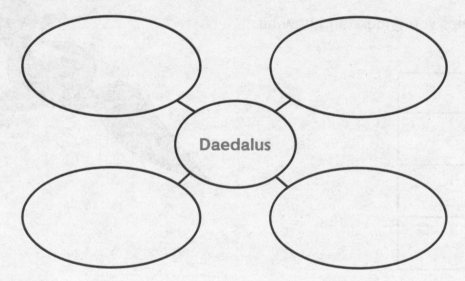

Daedalus

Write The author uses what Daedalus says and does to help me understand

_____

_____

_____

? How does the author use language to help you visualize what it was like for Icarus to fly?

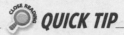

COLLABORATE

Talk About It Reread the first paragraph on page 155. With a partner, talk about Icarus's flight.

Cite Text Evidence What words or phrases help you visualize Icarus's flight? Write text evidence in the chart.

Text Evidence	What I Visualize

Write I can visualize what it was like for Icarus to fly because the author

_____

_____

_____

? How is the way the poet describes birds similar to the way the authors use words and phrases in *The Boy Who Drew Birds* and "Daedalus and Icarus"?

COLLABORATE

Talk About It Read the poem. With a partner, discuss what information you learned about swallows.

Cite Text Evidence Circle words and phrases in the poem that describe swallows. Draw a box around how the poet feels about the birds.

Write The way the poet describes birds is similar to the details in the selections because _____

_____

_____

_____

QUICK TIP

I see details in the poem that describe swallows. This will help me compare the poem to selections I read this week.

A Bird Song

It's a year almost that I have not seen her:
Oh, last summer green things were
    greener,
Brambles fewer, the blue sky bluer.

It's surely summer, for there's a swallow:
Come one swallow, his mate will follow,
The bird race quicken and wheel
    and thicken.

Oh happy swallow whose mate will follow
O'er height, o'er hollow! I'd be a swallow,
To build this weather one nest together.

— Christina Rossetti

U.S. Fish & Wildlife Service/Chelsi Hornbaker

Blancaflor

 How does the author use personification to set the tone of the story?

Literature Anthology: pages 156–169

Talk About It Reread page 157. Turn to your partner and discuss how the author describes the tree.

Cite Text Evidence What phrases describe the tree and set the mood of the folktale? Write text evidence in the chart.

Evidence	Mood

Write The author uses personification to _____

_____

Tip of the Week

When I **reread**, I can think about how the author uses words and phrases. I look for text evidence to answer questions.

Callie

Blend/Image Source

How does the author use descriptive language to help you visualize what the prince is experiencing?

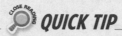 **QUICK TIP**

I can use these sentence frames when we discuss how the author creates the story's mood.

By using phrases such as . . .

The author makes me think of . . .

COLLABORATE

Talk About It Reread the first two paragraphs on page 161. Talk to a partner about how the author describes the landscape and what happens to the prince.

Cite Text Evidence What phrases create imagery? Use this web to record text evidence.

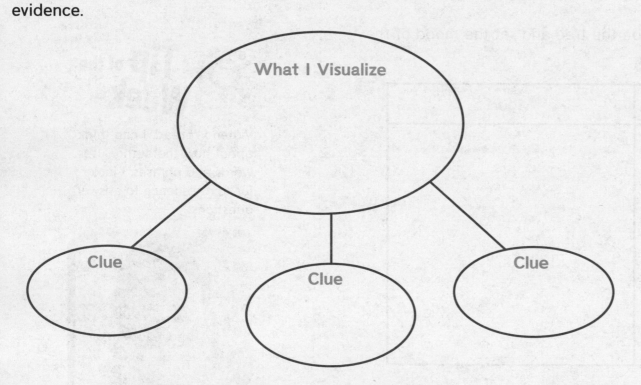

What I Visualize

Clue

Clue

Clue

Write I can visualize the setting because the author _____

_____

? **How does the author use words and phrases to change the tone of the story?**

Talk About It Reread paragraphs 4-6 on page 168. Turn to a partner and discuss how the tone of the story changes.

Cite Text Evidence What phrases mark the turning point of the story? Write them in the chart and how the tone changes.

Text Evidence	How It Changes Tone

Write The author changes the tone of the story by _____

_____

_____

 **QUICK TIP**

When I reread, I can think about how the author uses language to shift a story's mood or tone.

Your Turn

Think about how the author uses figurative language. How does the tone and mood change from the beginning of the folktale to the end? Use these sentence frames to help organize your text evidence.

The author sets the tone by...

She uses figurative language to show...

The mood changes because...

Go Digital!
Write your response online.

From Tale to Table

1. Whether it's a princess turning into a dove or a frog turning into a prince, many folktales and fairy tales include a magical transformation of one thing into another. Though it seems like an impossible task that only a magician could do, transformations can in fact happen in real life—even in your own kitchen!

A Wise Plan

2. Through the process of cooking and baking, individual ingredients can be transformed into something delicious. Did you know that the bread in the sandwich you had for lunch was probably made with only six basic ingredients: flour, water, oil, yeast, salt, and sugar? It may seem impossible, but by combining and heating these ingredients you can create something different: bread. It's not magic, but it does require a plan.

Reread and use the prompts to take notes in the text.

Reread paragraph 1. Circle clues that show what the author does to help you understand what a transformation is. Then underline what the author thinks of transformations. Write it here:

_____

_____

COLLABORATE

Reread paragraph 2. Talk with your partner about what you have to do to transform ingredients into bread. Write the numbers 1 to 6 beside each ingredient.

Then draw a box around what the author uses to foreshadow what information comes next.

Too Hot, Too Cold, and Just Right

1   A recipe has usually been tried and tested previously, so it is important to follow the steps carefully to get the same result. Slight changes in temperature can affect the outcome. For example, in step 1, the water should be warm, not hot. Why? Though it's hard to tell by looking at it, yeast is a living organism. At the right temperature, it gives off gases that create bubbles in the dough. This is what makes the dough rise. If you use hot water in the recipe, you can kill the yeast. If you use cold water, the yeast may create very little or no gas. Without the gas that the yeast produces, the dough will not rise.

Reread the excerpt. Underline what the author thinks is important to do when using a recipe. Circle something that might happen if you don't do it.

COLLABORATE

Talk with a partner about how the author uses cause and effect to organize information. Make a mark in the margin beside each cause-and-effect relationship in the paragraph. Write one of them here:

_____

_____

_____

Why is "From Tale to Table" a good title for this selection?

Talk About It Reread paragraph 1 on page 58. Talk with a partner about how the author introduces the selection and why that introduction is important.

Cite Text Evidence How does the author connect tales and recipes? Write text evidence in the chart.

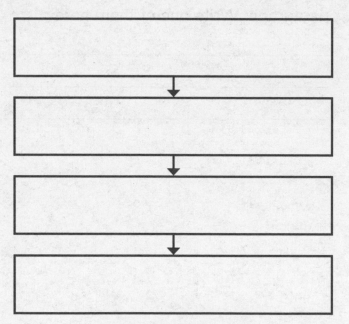

Write "From Tale to Table" is a good title for this selection because _____

_____

_____

 **QUICK TIP**

When I reread, I can pay close attention to details that connect information.

Dave King/Dorling Kindersley/Getty Images

Library of Congress Prints and Photographs Division [LC-USZ62-1277791]

? How do the Wright brothers and the authors of *Blancaflor* and "From Tale to Table" help you understand how plans can help people accomplish a task?

Talk About It Look at the sketches and read the caption. Talk with a partner about each image and what they tell you about the Wright brothers.

Cite Text Evidence Circle three things in the sketches that show how the Wright brothers planned to build their flying machine. Think about why the Wright brothers drew up these plans. In the margin beside each sketch, write words that describe the plans.

Write The Wright brothers and the authors show _____

_____

_____

_____

_____

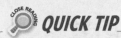

QUICK TIP

When I look at the sketches, I think about what they tell me about the people who created them. This helps me compare them to this week's selections.

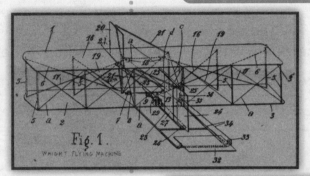

Fig. 1.
WRIGHT FLYING MACHINE

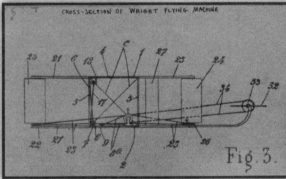

CROSS-SECTION OF WRIGHT FLYING MACHINE

Fig. 3.

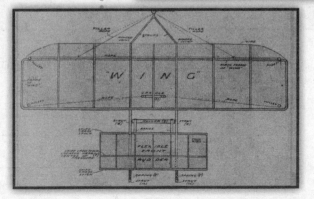

W I N G

The Wright brothers drew up these plans for their flying machine in 1908.

Stage Fright

How does the poet structure the poem to help you understand how the narrator feels before and after he performs?

Literature Anthology: pages 176–178

Talk About It Reread pages 176–177. Talk to your partner about how the poet sets the lines of the poem and how they relate to how the narrator feels.

Cite Text Evidence What does the poet do to help you visualize what the narrator is feeling? Write text evidence in the chart.

What the Poet Does	What I Visualize

Write The poet helps me understand how the narrator feels by _____

_____

_____

CLOSE READING

Tip of the Week

When I **reread**, I can use the way the poet uses structure to help me understand more about the poem.

Pete

KidStock/Blend Images/Getty Images

Catching Quiet

Why does the poet use repetition in "Catching Quiet"?

Talk About It Reread page 178. Turn to your partner and discuss the words and phrases the poet repeats.

Cite Text Evidence What words and phrases are repeated? Cite text evidence and explain why the author repeats them.

Words and Phrases	Author's Purpose

Write The poet uses repetition in "Catching Quiet" to _____

_____

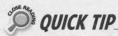

QUICK TIP

When I reread, I notice how the poet repeats certain words and phrases.

Your Turn

Think about the way both poems are organized. How do techniques like line arrangement and repetition help convey each poem's theme? Use these sentence frames to help organize your text evidence.

In "Stage Fright" the poet uses . . .

In "Catching Quiet" the poet . . .

Both techniques help me to . . .

Go Digital!
Write your response online.

Foul Shot

? How does the author use personification to help you understand how the boy feels?

COLLABORATE

Talk About It Reread page 180. Turn to your partner and talk about how the poet describes what the boy is feeling.

Cite Text Evidence What words and phrases paint a picture of how the boy feels? Write text evidence in the chart.

Personification	How the Boy Feels

Write The poet uses personification to help me understand _____

_____

_____

QUICK TIP

When I reread, I will use the way the author uses personification to help me understand more about how a character feels.

How does the poet's word choice create suspense in "Foul Shot?"

Talk About It Reread page 181. With a partner, talk about what happens when the boy lets the basketball go.

Cite Text Evidence What words and phrases create a feeling of suspense in the poem? Write text evidence in the web.

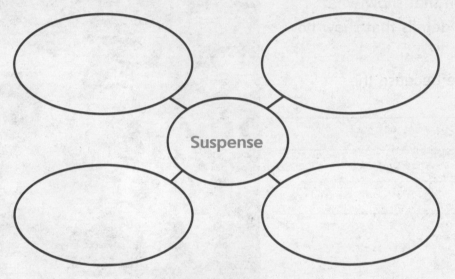

Suspense

Write The poet creates suspense by using words and phrases to _____

_____

_____

 **QUICK TIP**

When I reread, I can notice how the poet uses words and phrases to create suspense.

? How do the photographer and poets of "Stage Fright" and "Foul Shot" show how crowds or audiences affect performance?

COLLABORATE

Talk About It Look at the photograph and read the caption. With a partner, discuss whether you think the crowd affects the way Althea Gibson plays tennis.

Cite Text Evidence Underline clues in the photograph that show what might affect Althea Gibson as she plays tennis. Circle details that show how she feels.

Write I can see how a crowd can affect performance because the

photographer and poets _____

_____

_____

Popperfoto/Getty Images

Althea Gibson was the first African-American tennis player to compete at Wimbledon. She won in 1957 and 1958.

They Don't Mean It!

Literature Anthology: pages 182–193

? How does the author show that Mary's mother does not feel like she is being true to her culture?

COLLABORATE

Talk About It Reread paragraph 5 on page 184. Turn to a partner and talk about how Mary describes her mother.

Cite Text Evidence What clues show that Mary's mother is not keeping her Chinese traditions? Write text evidence in the chart.

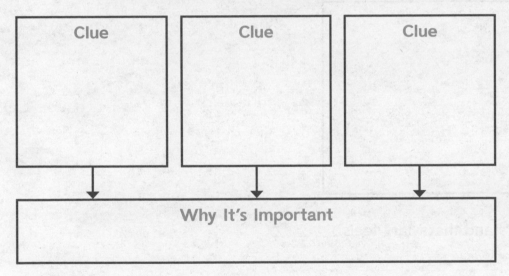

Clue	Clue	Clue

Why It's Important

Write I know that Mary's mother feels like she is not being true to her culture because the author _____

_____

CLOSE READING Tip of the Week

When I **reread**, I can think about how the author describes what characters do. This helps me understand how they feel.

Chen

Yobro10/iStock/360/Getty Images

? How does the author use dialogue to help you understand how Mary feels about American customs?

COLLABORATE

Talk About It Reread paragraphs 4 and 5 on page 187. Turn to a partner and talk about what Mary is worried about.

Cite Text Evidence What does Mary say and how does it show how she feels? Write text evidence in the chart.

Text Evidence	What It Shows

Write The author uses dialogue to help me understand that Mary feels _____

_____

_____

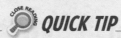

QUICK TIP

I can use these sentence frames when we talk about how Mary feels.

The author shows that Mary is worried about . . .

I read that dessert is . . .

? **How does the author use the illustration to show how Mrs. Yang has changed?**

COLLABORATE

Talk About It Reread the fifth paragraph on page 193. With a partner, use clues from the text and illustration to talk about what Mrs. Yang does.

Cite Text Evidence What clues in the text and illustration help you see how Mrs. Yang has changed? Write evidence in the chart.

Text Evidence	Illustration Clues	What It Shows

Write The author uses the illustration to show that Mrs. Yang has changed

by _____

_____

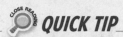

QUICK TIP
When I **reread**, I can use the illustrations to help me learn more about the characters.

Your Turn

How does the author show how the Yangs change as they try to find a balance between their Chinese traditions and their new American life? Use the sentence frames to help organize your text evidence.

The author uses dialogue to show . . .

The illustrations help me to see . . .

This helps me understand how the Yangs . . .

Go Digital!
Write your response online.

Where Did That Come From?

From Bite...

[1]   Food is one of the most common ways people have shared cultures. Dishes we think of as American have in fact come from all over the world. Hamburgers were crafted by German immigrants. Macaroni was rolled out by Italians. Apple pie was first served not in America but England.

...To Beat

[2]   People from different backgrounds have also drummed distinct sounds into the music we hear today. Hip hop and rap, for example, have been traced to West African and Caribbean storytelling. Salsa music comes from a type of Cuban music called "son," which has been linked to both Spanish and African cultures. These unique genres owe their rhythms to the drum. This instrument can be found in nearly every culture in the world.

Reread and use the prompts to take notes in the text.

Reread the first heading. Underline clues in paragraph 1 that show this is a good heading for the section.

COLLABORATE

Reread the second heading. Talk about how the author shows that both paragraphs are related. Circle what the author does to help you see that.

In paragraph 2, draw a box around the sentence that helps you understand the heading. How does the author support his choice for the heading? Circle the text evidence. Write it here:

1. _____

2. _____

3. _____

United in Sports

3   Even the sports we play have come from other places. Soccer's origins have been connected with a number of countries, including Italy and China. Tennis likely came from France, but some think it may have even been played in ancient Egypt. While no one may know the exact origin of some of these sports, there is no doubt they are now considered popular American activities.

4   Our nation has been enriched by a diversity of cultures. Learning the origins of what makes up American culture can lead to a new appreciation for the people and places from which they came.

Reread the excerpt. Circle two examples the author uses to support the heading of this section.

COLLABORATE

Talk with a partner about why "United in Sports" is a good heading. Make a mark in the margin beside the text evidence that supports your discussion.

Reread paragraph 4. Underline two benefits of diversity in our country. Write them here:

1. _____

2. _____

How do the headings help you understand the influence of other cultures on America?

QUICK TIP

When I **reread**, I can use headings to help me understand the topic.

Talk About It Reread the headings on pages 70–71. With a partner, talk about how they are related and what the author wants you to understand.

Cite Text Evidence What text evidence shows that the headings and text are related? Write it in the chart.

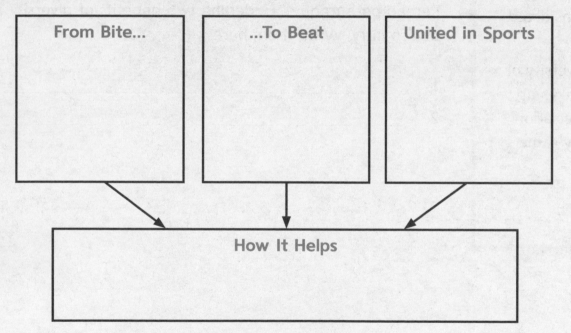

From Bite...	...To Beat	United in Sports

How It Helps

Write The headings help me understand _____

_____

_____

_____

? How do Frances Frost and the authors of *They Don't Mean It!* and "Where Did That Come From?" help you understand their messages about other cultures?

COLLABORATE

Talk About It With a partner, read the song lyrics. Talk about why Frances Frost wrote the song in two languages.

Cite Text Evidence Circle clues in the song that tell what the singer is doing. Underline details that show the result of the singer's actions. Draw a box around the songwriter's reason for taking action. Think about what the songwriter wants you to know.

Write The songwriter and authors share their messages by _____

_____

_____

_____

_____

_____

George Doyle/SuperStock

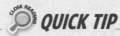
QUICK TIP

I see the song is written in both Portuguese and English. This will help me compare it to the selections I read this week.

De Lanterna na Mão
(With a Lantern in My Hand)

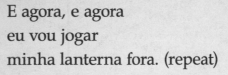

Eu procurei,
de lanterna na mão,
procurei, procurei, e achei
Você para o meu coração.
(repeat)

E agora, e agora
eu vou jogar
minha lanterna fora. (repeat)

I search for you with a lantern in my hand.
Searching here, searching there
and at last I find you, and you are my friend.
(repeat)

I have found you, I have found you
and now I can throw away my lantern.
(repeat)

— Frances Frost

Reread

Weslandia

? How does the author use dialogue to help you understand Wesley's motives?

COLLABORATE

Talk About It Reread page 202. Turn to your partner and talk about what Wesley's father says.

Cite Text Evidence What words and phrases help you understand how Wesley reacts to his father's remarks? Use text evidence to support your response.

What Wesley Hears	Why It's Important

Write The author uses dialogue to help me understand how Wesley _____

_____

_____

Literature Anthology: pages 198–211

Tip of the Week

When I **reread**, I can use dialogue to help me understand what characters do. I look for text evidence to answer questions.

Miguel

? **How does the author help you see how Wesley's schoolmates have changed?**

COLLABORATE

Talk About It Reread paragraph 5 on page 207. Talk with a partner about how the text and illustration help you know more about Wesley's schoolmates.

Cite Text Evidence What details in the text and illustration help you understand what Wesley's schoolmates do? Write evidence in the chart.

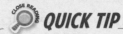

QUICK TIP

I can use these sentence frames when we talk about Wesley's schoolmates.

I read that Wesley's schoolmates are now . . .

The author uses the illustration to show . . .

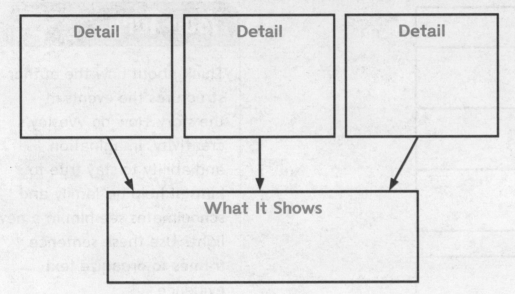

Detail	Detail	Detail

What It Shows

Write The author helps me see the change in Wesley's schoolmates by _____

_____

_____

? **How do you know Wesley's parents are impressed with his project?**

Talk About It Reread page 210. Turn to a partner and talk about what Wesley's parents say to him.

Cite Text Evidence What clues help you know that Wesley's parents are impressed? Write them in the chart.

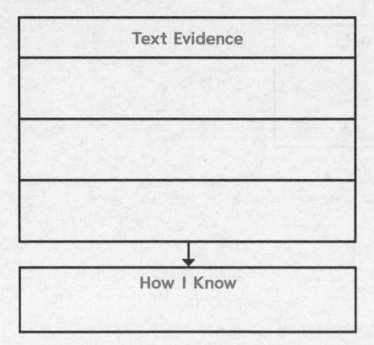

Text Evidence

↓

How I Know

Write I know that Wesley's parents are impressed because the author _____

_____

_____

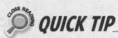 **QUICK TIP**

When I **reread**, I can use the way the author shows how characters interact to understand how they change.

Your Turn

Think about how the author structures the events in the story. How do Wesley's creativity, imagination, and ability to stay true to himself help his family and schoolmates see him in a new light? Use these sentence frames to organize text evidence.

The author organizes the story . . .

He uses dialogue to . . .

This shows me how Wesley . . .

Go Digital!
Write your response online.

Plants with a Purpose

One Plant, Many Uses

1.   Some resourceful people have found numerous ways to use a plant that grows well in their region. Bamboo, for example, is a type of plant originally from tropical parts of the world. Bamboo can grow quickly and closely together. This makes it a useful crop. People can cook and eat bamboo shoots. Yet bamboo in its raw form is a very strong building material. It is used to construct fences, bridges, and homes. People can use it to weave baskets and mats. They have even developed a process to soften bamboo to make cloth.

2.   Corn, a plant from the western hemisphere, has a variety of uses too. Corn is a staple food crop and used to feed livestock. Additionally, it is made into fuel, plastic, and textiles.

Reread and use the prompts to take notes in the text.

Circle text evidence in paragraph 1 that shows what the author thinks of people who use plants in many ways. Write it here:

_____

In the margin beside paragraph 1, number the ways people use bamboo.

Reread paragraph 2. Talk about how corn can be used. Underline text evidence that supports your discussion.

Plants Inspire Invention

3 Plants have also been used as models to make new materials. For example, rubber is a manufactured material that is based on a substance that comes from a tree. The rubber tree oozes a sap that can be processed to make it very durable and flexible. By studying the plant's sap, scientists figured out a way to make rubber on their own. About 70% of all rubber used today is now made by humans. But without these unique trees, we might never have created this useful material.

Replacing What We Use

4 We cultivate plants to meet many different needs. So it is important that we do not use them up or overuse the land on which they are grown. Plants that are harvested should be replaced. Crops should be rotated so that nutrients in the soil that are used up can be restored. By following these practices, we ensure the survival of living things and provide opportunities for more innovating uses.

Reread paragraph 3. Circle an example of how the author helps you understand how plants inspire invention.

COLLABORATE

Reread paragraph 4. Talk with a partner about how the author feels about plants. Underline text evidence that shows what the author thinks.

Why is "Replacing What We Use" a good heading for this section? Use text evidence in your answer.

_____

_____

_____

How does the author feel about replacing the plants we use?

COLLABORATE

Talk About It Reread the excerpt on page 78. With a partner, discuss why you think the author gives you advice about how to take care of plants.

Cite Text Evidence What details in the text tell you the author's point of view about replacing plants? Write evidence in the chart.

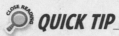 **QUICK TIP**

When I **reread**, I can use text evidence to understand the author's point of view.

Text Evidence	Author's Point of View

Write I know how the author feels about replacing plants because she _____

_____

_____

? How is the way Emily Dickinson describes a bird similar to the way the authors of *Weslandia* and "Plants with a Purpose" use words and phrases to help you understand how learning about nature can be useful?

COLLABORATE

Talk About It Read the poem. With a partner, talk about what Emily Dickinson had to do to write her poem. Compare it to what Wesley did before and while he created Weslandia.

Cite Text Evidence Circle words and phrases in the poem that show what the bird is doing. Think about how the poet and authors of the selections you read this week show how learning about nature is useful.

Write Emily Dickinson and the authors help me understand how

learning about nature can be useful by _____

_____

_____

_____

_____

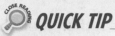

A Bird Came Down the Walk

A bird came down the walk:
He did not know I saw;
He bit an angle-worm in halves
And ate the fellow, raw.

And then he drank a dew
From a convenient grass,
And then hopped sidewise to the wall
To let a beetle pass.

— Emily Dickinson

USFWS Pacific Southwest Region

The Story of Snow

? How does the author use captions to create more interest in snow crystals?

Talk About It Look at the photographs and read the captions on pages 220–221. Talk with a partner about what they help you understand.

Cite Text Evidence What information do the photographs and captions show that the main text does not state? Write text evidence and how it helps.

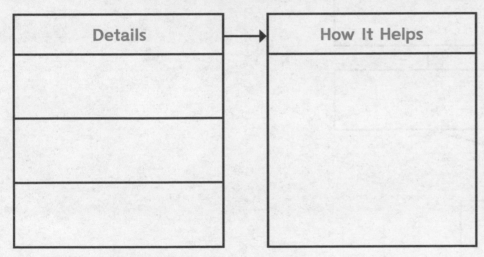

Details	How It Helps

Write The author uses photographs and captions to _____

_____

_____

Literature Anthology: pages 216–229

Tip of the Week

When I **reread**, I can use photographs and captions to understand more about the topic. I find text evidence to answer questions.

Samantha

How does the author organize the information to help you understand more about snow crystals?

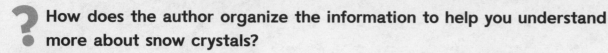

Talk About It Look at pages 222–223. Talk with a partner about the way the author organizes information and what you learned.

Cite Text Evidence What does the author do to organize the information about snow crystals? Write evidence in the chart.

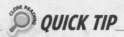

How the Author Organizes Text

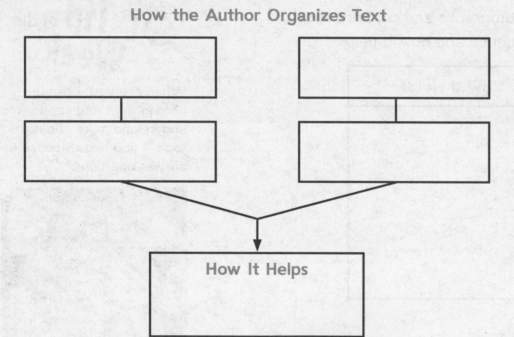

How It Helps

Write The author organizes information about snow crystals by _____

_____

_____

? **How does the author use captions to create more interest in snow crystals?**

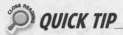 **QUICK TIP**

When I reread, I can use captions to learn more about the topic.

Talk About It Reread the caption on page 227. Talk with a partner about how the author describes how you can see a snow crystal.

Cite Text Evidence What does the author do in the caption on page 227? Write text evidence in the chart.

Text Evidence	What It Shows

Write The author uses the caption to create more interest by _____

_____

_____

Your Turn

How does the way Mark Cassino presents information help you understand snow crystals? Use these sentence frames to organize text evidence.

Mark Cassino organizes information by . . .

He uses text features to . . .

This helps me understand . . .

Go Digital!
Write your response online.

Fibonacci's Amazing Find

1   What do the numbers 1, 1, 2, 3, 5, 8, 13, 21, and 34 have in common? These are the first numbers in the Fibonacci sequence, a series of numbers calculated over 800 years ago by a mathematician named Fibonacci. But that's not all they have in common. These numbers also can be found in nature. They can be found, for example, in the number of petals of flowers.

Black-eyed Susan: 13 petals

Buttercup: 5 petals

Iris: 3 petals

Reread and use the prompts to take notes in the text.

Underline how the author helps you understand what Fibonacci's sequence is.

COLLABORATE

Talk with a partner about where you can see examples of Fibonacci's sequence. Circle clues in the text and photographs that support your discussion.

How does the way the author begins the selection make you want to read more? Draw a box around the sentence.

Field Daisy: 34 petals

Numbers from the Fibonacci sequence can be found in the numbers of petals of many flowers.

1   Centuries later, people noticed these numbers in nature. Naturalists found that the growth pattern of some living things reflected Fibonacci numbers. For example, the chambered nautilus, a type of marine animal, adds a new chamber to its shell as it grows. Each additional chamber is the same shape as the previous one, but larger in size. This maintains the shell's overall shape. The diagram and directions below illustrate how this type of growth can produce a pattern that reflects the Fibonacci sequence.

Circle how the author helps you understand what the chambered nautilus is. Make marks in the margin that point to how you know the chambered nautilus maintains its shell's overall shape.

COLLABORATE

Talk with a partner about how the diagram helps you understand what the text describes. Number each chamber in the diagram beginning with the smallest ones.

Read the caption and look at the photograph. Underline evidence in the caption that tells about the inside of the shell. Trace the spiral shape of the shell.

The cross-section of a chambered nautilus shell reveals a repetition of curves and a spiral shape.

Seth Joel Photography/Cultura/Getty Images

? **What does the author do to help you understand the Fibonacci sequence?**

COLLABORATE

Talk About It Reread the excerpts on pages 84–85. Talk about what helps you understand Fibonacci's sequence.

Cite Text Evidence How does the author present the information? Write evidence in the web.

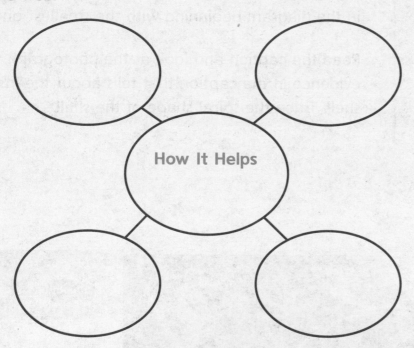

How It Helps

Write The author helps me understand Fibonacci's sequence by _____

_____

_____

QUICK TIP

When I reread, I can use text features to help me understand the topic.

? **How is the way Vincent Van Gogh uses patterns in the painting similar to the patterns you read about in *The Story of Snow* and "Fibonacci's Amazing Find"?**

COLLABORATE

Talk About It With a partner, look at the painting. Read the caption. Talk about how the flower beds make patterns.

Cite Text Evidence Draw lines to separate the rows and columns in the painting.

Write The way Van Gogh uses patterns is similar to the patterns in the selections because _____

_____

_____

_____

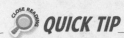
QUICK TIP

I see a simple pattern in the painting. This will help me compare the painting to the selections I read this week.

Courtesy National Gallery of Art, Washington

Dutch painter Vincent van Gogh painted *Flower Beds in Holland* in 1883. It is an oil on canvas painting.

Winter's Tail

Literature Anthology:
pages 236–249

? How do you know that the aquarium staff is concerned about Winter?

COLLABORATE

Talk About It Reread paragraphs 2 and 3 on page 240. Look at the photograph. Talk with a partner about how the staff helps Winter when she arrives at the aquarium.

Cite Text Evidence What evidence shows how the trainers feel about Winter? Write it in the chart.

Text Evidence	Photograph Clues	What It Shows

Write I know that the aquarium staff is concerned about Winter because the

authors _____

_____

_____

Tip of the Week

When I **reread**, I can use text and photographs to help me understand more about the topic. I find text evidence to answer questions.

Yolanda

Sandy Jones/Stockbyte/Getty Images

? How do the authors help you visualize what the team had to think about while creating Winter's prosthesis?

COLLABORATE

Talk About It Reread the last paragraph on page 245. Turn to a partner and talk about what the team had to consider as they created the prosthesis.

Cite Text Evidence What words and phrases help you picture what the team did? Write text evidence in the chart.

Text Evidence	What I Visualize

Write I can visualize how the team created the prothesis because the author

_____

_____

QUICK TIP

I can use these sentence frames when we talk about the team.

The authors use words and phrases to help me understand that the team . . .

This helps me see that . . .

How do the authors show how Winter will continue to have an impact on the people who helped her?

 **QUICK TIP**

When I reread, I can use the authors' words and phrases to help me understand how people work together to help animals.

COLLABORATE

Talk About It Reread the second paragraph on page 249. Turn to a partner and discuss what the team will need to do.

Cite Text Evidence How do you know that the team will continue helping Winter? Write text evidence in the chart.

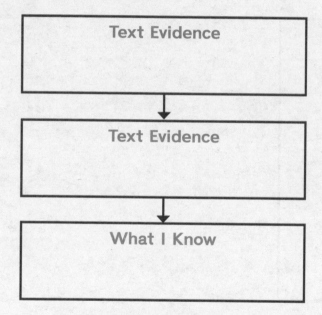

Text Evidence

↓

Text Evidence

↓

What I Know

Write I know that Winter will continue to be a part of her team's lives because

_____

_____

_____

Your Turn

How do the authors help you understand how many people have been inspired by Winter's story? Use these sentence frames to organize text evidence.

The authors show that the aquarium staff . . .

They tell about people who . . .

This helps me understand how Winter . . .

Go Digital!
Write your response online.

Helping Hands

A Need Inspires

[1] The rules of the competition asked participants to come up with new and innovative ways to help heal, repair or improve the human body. One of the group members, Kate Murray, understood the difficulties people with an injury or impairment can face. Kate was born with a left hand that was not fully formed. But that didn't stop Kate from taking part in activities. When she decided she wanted to learn how to play the violin, she and her mother worked with a team of specialists to create a device to allow her to hold a bow.

[2] The Flying Monkeys wondered if they could create something similar for the competition. When one of their Girl Scouts coaches learned about Danielle Fairchild, a three-year-old who was born without fingers on her right hand, the Flying Monkeys found their inspiration.

Reread and use the prompts to take notes in the text.

Underline why Kate Murray understands how people with an injury or impairment feel.

Circle clues that help you understand what Kate is like.

COLLABORATE

Reread paragraph 2. Talk with a partner about how the Flying Monkeys found their inspiration. Make a mark in the margin beside the text evidence.

Why is "A Need Inspires" a good heading for this section? Use text evidence to write your answer here:

_____

_____

Introducing the BOB-1

1   Before long, the Flying Monkeys settled on a final design for their invention, which they called the BOB-1. They used a flexible plastic substance, a pencil grip, and hook-and-eye closures to build it. Everyone involved was impressed by how well the device would fit on Danielle's hand. What's more, it was very simple and inexpensive to make. Why hadn't anyone thought of creating a device like this before?

2   The Flying Monkeys created fliers, a portfolio, and even a skit to take to the competition and showcase their invention. The competition judges were impressed.

3   The Flying Monkeys won a regional and state-level innovation award. From there, it was on to the global round of the contest, where the BOB-1 would be judged alongside 178 other entries from 16 countries. The winning team would receive $20,000 to further develop the product.

In paragraph 1, underline how the author describes the BOB-1.

Reread paragraph 2. Circle what the group did to impress the judges at the competition. Write text evidence here:

1. _____

2. _____

3. _____

COLLABORATE

Reread paragraph 3. Talk about what happened at the competition and where the Flying Monkeys were headed next. Draw a box around how the author helps you understand the word *global*.

? How does the author organize the information to help you understand what the Flying Monkeys did to create BOB-1?

Talk About It Look back at your annotations on pages 91–92. With a partner, talk about how the author organizes the information to help you understand what the Flying Monkeys do.

Cite Text Evidence What are the ways the author organizes the text? Write them here.

How the Author Organizes the Text	

Write I use the way the author organizes information to help me understand

_____

_____

 **QUICK TIP**

When I reread, I can use the way the author organizes information to help me understand the text.

? How do advances in technology allow these firefighters and the teams described in *Winter's Tail* and "Helping Hands" to help others?

COLLABORATE

Talk About It Look at the lithograph. Read the caption. The water pumps in the picture are steam powered. This was new technology at the time. Talk with a partner about what the firefighters are doing.

Cite Text Evidence Draw a box around the details that show the water pumps are steam powered. Circle as many different jobs you see the firefighters doing.

Write I see how advances in technology help others

_____

_____

_____

_____

_____

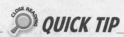 **QUICK TIP**

I see how steam power helped the firefighters do their jobs better. This will help me compare text to art.

Library of Congress Prints and Photographs Division [LC-DIG-pga-00811]

The Life of a Fireman: The New Era. Steam and Muscle was created in 1861 by American illustrator Charles Parsons. It was printed by Currier & Ives.

Machu Picchu: Ancient City

? How does the author organize the information to help you understand his point of view?

Literature Anthology:
pages 256–259

COLLABORATE

Talk About It Reread "A Reasonable Retreat" on page 257. Turn to your partner and talk about how the author builds information to support his opinion.

Cite Text Evidence What words and phrases does the author use to organize the information? Write text evidence in the chart.

CLOSE READING

Tip of the Week

When I **reread**, I use how the author organizes information to help me understand his point of view. I can find text evidence to answer questions.

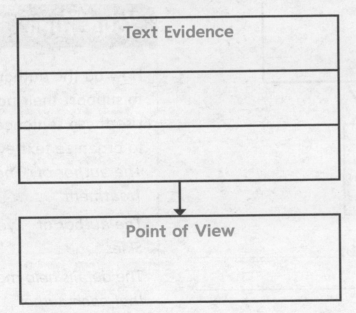

Text Evidence

↓

Point of View

Marta

Write The author organizes the information to share his point of view by _____

_____

How does the author help you visualize the Temple of the Sun?

COLLABORATE

Talk About It Reread the fourth paragraph on page 258. Turn to your partner and describe what the Temple of the Sun is like.

Cite Text Evidence What words and phrases help you visualize what the Temple of the Sun looks like? Write text evidence in the chart.

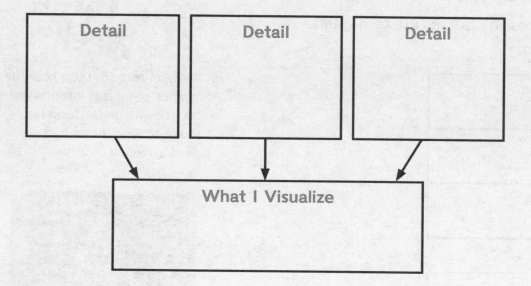

Detail	Detail	Detail

What I Visualize

Write The author helps me visualize the Temple of the Sun by _____

_____

_____

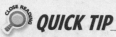 **QUICK TIP**

I can use the author's words and phrases to help me visualize.

Your Turn

How do the authors use details to support their positions? Use these sentence frames to organize text evidence.

The author of "The Royal Treatment" . . .

The author of "Eyes on the Skies" . . .

The details help me understand that each author . . .

Go Digital!
Write your response online.

Dig This Technology!

1   Another tool archaeologists use is a device that looks like a lawn mower. Called "ground penetrating radar" (GPR), it uses radar to locate artifacts under the ground. Radar bounces radio waves off an object to show its location. The diagram below shows how GPR helps archaeologists find artifacts.

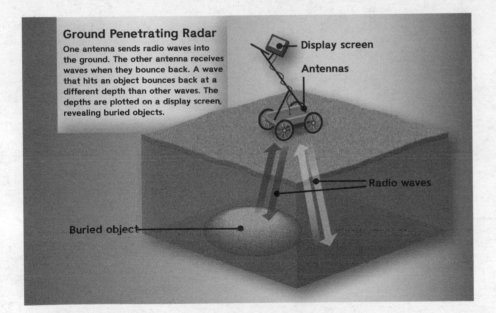

Ground Penetrating Radar
One antenna sends radio waves into the ground. The other antenna receives waves when they bounce back. A wave that hits an object bounces back at a different depth than other waves. The depths are plotted on a display screen, revealing buried objects.

Display screen

Antennas

Radio waves

Buried object

Reread and use the prompts to take notes in the text.

Circle how the author describes the ground penetrating radar to help you understand what it looks like. Underline what the GPR does.

COLLABORATE

Look at the diagram. Talk with a partner about what the caption describes and what you see in the diagram. How does this help you understand more about what the GPR does? Use text evidence to write your response here:

_____

_____

_____

? How does the diagram help you understand how scientists find and analyze artifacts?

COLLABORATE

Talk About It Reread the excerpt on page 97 and look at the diagram. With a partner, talk about what the diagram shows.

Cite Text Evidence What clues in the diagram help you understand how it helps scientists find and analyze buried artifacts? Write evidence in the chart.

Evidence	How It Helps

Write The diagram helps me understand _____

_____

_____

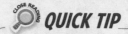

COLLABORATE

? How do the photographer and the authors of "Machu Picchu: Ancient City" and "Dig This Technology!" help you understand how people learn about the past by reconstructing and researching it?

Talk About It Look at the photograph. Read the caption. Talk with a partner about what the paleontologist is doing.

Cite Text Evidence Draw a box around clues in the photograph that show what Dr. Ross is doing. Circle some of the things he does to recreate the skeleton. In the caption, underline text evidence that explains what he is preparing the skeleton for.

Write I understand how reconstructing and researching the past helps people learn more because _____

_____

_____

_____

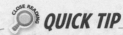
QUICK TIP

I see clues in the photograph that help me understand how we learn about the past. This will help me compare it to the selections I read this week.

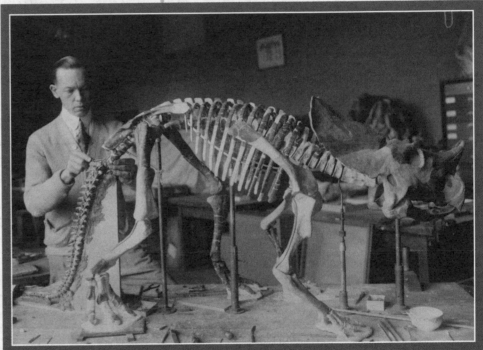

Norman Ross, a paleontologist, prepares a skeleton of a baby dinosaur for an exhibit. Ross worked at the National Museum in 1921.

Davy Crockett Saves the World

Literature Anthology: pages 262–275

? How does the author's use of personification add humor to the story?

COLLABORATE

Talk About It Reread the first paragraph on page 265. Turn to your partner and discuss how the author describes Halley's Comet.

Cite Text Evidence What words and phrases show how the comet has human characteristics? Write text evidence in the chart and tell why it's funny.

Text Evidence	How This Adds Humor

CLOSE READING

Tip of the Week

When I **reread**, I can think about how the author uses personification. I look for text evidence to answer questions.

Write The author uses personification to add humor to the story by _____

_____

Karim

Image Source/Getty Images

? **Why does the author exaggerate Davy Crockett's behavior?**

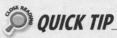
COLLABORATE

Talk About It Reread the third and fourth paragraphs on page 269. Talk with a partner about how the author describes Davy Crockett.

Cite Text Evidence What words and phrases show that the author is exaggerating? Cite text evidence and explain why the author uses it.

Text Evidence	Author's Purpose

Write The author exaggerates Davy's character because _____

_____

_____

QUICK TIP

I can use these sentence frames when we talk about how the author uses exaggeration.

The author describes Davy Crockett using words like . . .

This helps me picture . . .

? How does the author's use of sensory language help you visualize what Davy does with the comet?

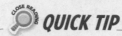

QUICK TIP

I can use the author's sensory language to create an image in my mind.

Talk About It Reread the second paragraph on page 272. Turn to a partner and talk about what Davy does with the comet.

Cite Text Evidence What words does the author use to help you picture Davy and the comet? Write text evidence in the web.

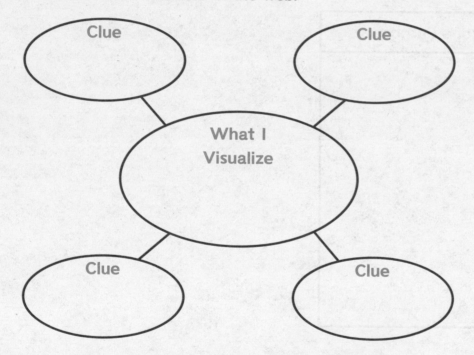

Write The author helps me visualize what Davy Crockett does with the

comet by _____

_____

_____

Your Turn

Think about how the author uses literary devices. What effect do these techniques have on the story? Use these sentence frames to organize your text evidence.

The author uses personification to . . .

The way she exaggerates events helps me to see . . .

The sensory language she uses makes the story . . .

Go Digital!
Write your response online.

How Grandmother Spider Stole the Sun

 Why is it important to the story that two animals tried and were not able to steal the Sun?

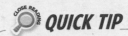
Talk About It Reread page 279. Turn to your partner and discuss what happens before Grandmother Spider tries to steal the Sun.

Cite Text Evidence What happens to the first two animals who try to steal the Sun? Write text evidence in the chart.

Text Evidence	What It Tells Me

Write It is important that two animals were not able to steal the Sun

because _____

_____

_____

_____

_____

Unit 4 · Week 1 · Sharing Stories   **103**

How does the author's use of repetition help you understand what Buzzard is like?

Talk About It Reread the second paragraph on page 280. Turn to your partner and talk about what Buzzard does.

Cite Text Evidence What words and phrases are repeated? Write text evidence and tell why it's important.

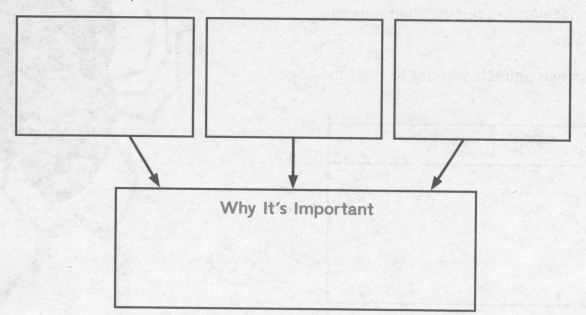

Why It's Important

Write The author uses repetition to help me understand _____

_____

_____

QUICK TIP

I can use these sentence frames when we talk about how the author uses repetition.

The author repeats the words and phrases . . .

This helps me know that Buzzard is . . .

How does the author's use of sensory language help you understand the legend's theme?

 **QUICK TIP**

When I **reread**, I think about how the author uses words and phrases to tell what the characters do. This helps me figure out the theme, or message.

COLLABORATE

Talk About It Reread page 281. Talk with a partner about what the different animals did.

Cite Text Evidence What message does the author want you to know? Cite text evidence in the chart and write the theme.

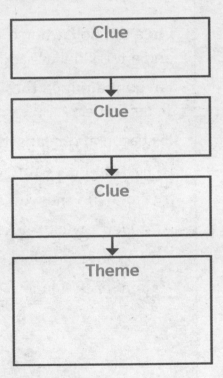

Clue
↓
Clue
↓
Clue
↓
Theme

Write The author helps me understand the legend's theme by _____

_____

_____

? How does the songwriter help you visualize the song and how is it similar to the way the authors tell their stories in *Davy Crockett Saves the World* and "How Grandmother Spider Stole the Sun"?

Talk About It Read the song lyrics. Talk with a partner about what the song is about. Choose a phrase and discuss how the writer helps you picture what's happening.

Cite Text Evidence Underline phrases that show how the subject of the song tells about what he will do. Circle words that help you visualize the story. Think about how the authors use words and phrases in the stories you read this week to help you visualize.

Write The songwriter and authors help me visualize the stories they tell by _____

_____

_____

_____

_____

_____

QUICK TIP
The lyrics helps me visualize the song. This will help me compare the song to text.

The Old Chisholm Trail

On a ten dollar horse
and a forty dollar saddle,
I'm gonna punch those
Texas cattle.
It's bacon and beans 'most ev'ry day.
I'd as soon be a-eatin' prairie hay.
It's cloudy in the west and it looks like rain,
And I left my old slicker in the wagon again.
I'm gonna see the boss, gonna get my money,
   Goin' back home to see my honey.

©Mick Roessler/Corbis

A Window Into History

? How does the author show that people have different points of view about turning Grandma J.'s house into a playground?

Literature Anthology: pages 282–291

Talk About It Reread page 285. Turn to a partner and discuss why Daniel Cruz asks everyone what they think about the playground.

Cite Text Evidence What words and phrases tell how each character feels about the house being turned into a playground? Write text evidence in the chart.

Text Evidence	What It Shows

Write The author shows that people have different point of views by _____

_____

Tip of the Week

When I **reread**, I can think about how the author uses words and phrases to tell the character's point of view. I look for text evidence to answer questions.

Reggie

Unit 4 · Week 2 · Discoveries **107**

How does the author build suspense?

QUICK TIP

I can use these sentence frames when we talk about how the author builds suspense.

The author describes . . .

This makes me feel . . .

Talk About It Reread Act 2, Scene 2 on page 288. Turn to a partner and talk about how the details in this scene build suspense.

Cite Text Evidence What details in this scene add to the suspense? Use evidence from the text to support your answers.

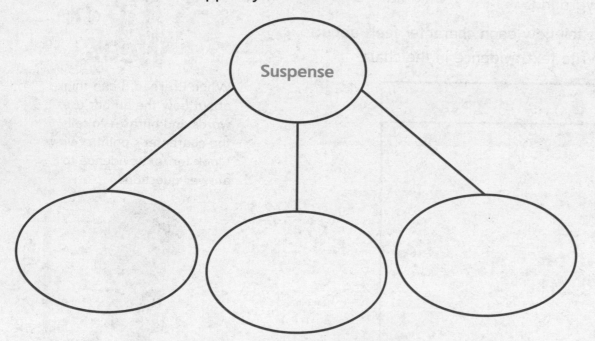

Suspense

Write The author builds suspense in this scene by _____

_____

_____

Why does the author have Daniel Cruz interview Dr. Cedric Brown about the history of the house?

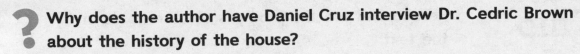

Talk About It Reread pages 290 and 291. Turn to a partner and talk about what Dr. Cedric Brown says.

Cite Text Evidence What words and phrases show that Dr. Cedric Brown's interview is important? Write text evidence in the chart.

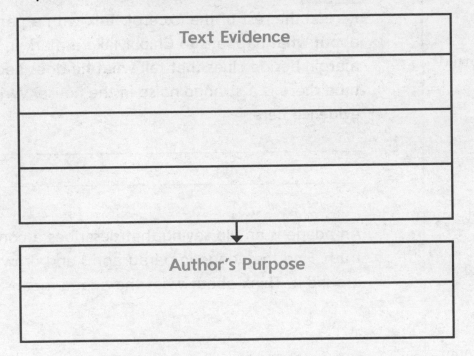

Text Evidence

↓

Author's Purpose

Write I know Dr. Cedric Brown's interview is important because _____

_____

_____

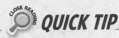
Your Turn

Think about Daniel Cruz's role as a reporter. How does the author use his interviews to help you understand the events in the play? Use these sentence frames to organize your text evidence.

The author uses Daniel Cruz to . . .

The interviews help the author to . . .

They help me understand . . .

Go Digital!
Write your response online.

A Second Chance for Chip

[1]   When we noticed last winter that Chip was gaining weight, my mom said, "He needs more exercise." Mom coaches soccer, and exercise is her solution to everything. She reasoned that a dog door between the kitchen and the backyard might help, so this past spring, she purchased a do-it-yourself kit and I offered my assistance. "Many hands make light work," Mom declared. We started building.

[2]   Pounding in the kitchen? Under the bed.

[3]   After the door's installation, Chip slimmed down considerably–twenty pounds, to be precise. That sounds like success, but the vet was suspicious. "He's underweight now," the vet reported. "Is he eating well?"

[4]   "He eats plenty," I replied. "I fill his bowl every night, and every morning it's empty."

[5]   "He doesn't eat immediately?" the vet asked.

[6]   "I guess he waits till everyone's asleep," my mom said, offering an explanation. "He is afraid of the noise of the dishwasher." Gurgling dishwasher? Under the bed.

Reread and use the prompts to take notes in the text.

Underline Mom's solution in paragraph 1 to Chip's weight gain. Circle words and phrases that help you know what Mom is like.

COLLABORATE

Reread the rest of the excerpt. Talk with a partner about what happens to Chip. Make a mark in the margin beside clues that tell what he does each time there is a strange noise in the house. Write text evidence here:

_____

_____

An adage is an old saying that describes a common truth. Find the adage in paragraph 1 and draw a box around it. Think about what the adage means.

1   "Are you suggesting that Mrs. Stenforth is wrong?"

2   "She's never even met Chip," I said. A neighbor knocks or rings the bell? Under the bed.

3   I tapped Chip's door with my foot, and it swung. Surprised that it responded to such light pressure, I looked more closely and then noticed scratch marks in the paint—marks that looked too tiny to be Chip's. But Chip was our only pet. Could something else be causing all this trouble? I'd have to investigate.

4   That night, I tucked a flashlight under my pillow and waited. Around midnight, I heard Chip's toenails click across the floor, then creaking steps as he crept downstairs. A minute later, his dog door swished open and shut. I slipped out of bed with my flashlight, but before I could take another step, Chip came barreling up the stairs and dove under the bed.

Reread paragraphs 1 and 2. Circle what happens when Chip hears a neighbor knock or ring the bell.

Write text evidence here:

_____

_____

COLLABORATE

Reread paragraphs 3 and 4. Talk with a partner about how the author uses words and phrases to create suspense. Underline text evidence that supports your discussion.

? **Why does the author repeat the phrase "under the bed" throughout the story?**

Talk About It Reread the excerpts. With a partner, discuss why the author gives examples of how frightened Chip is of loud noises.

Cite Text Evidence What words and phrases help you understand what Chip is afraid of? Write text evidence in the chart.

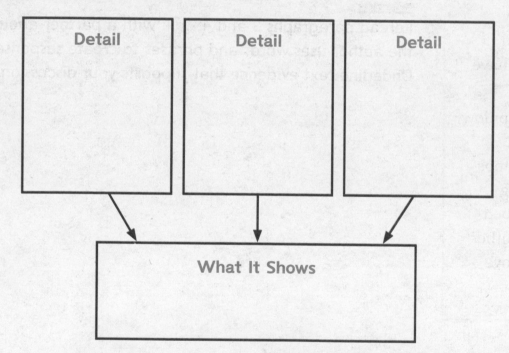

Detail

Detail

Detail

What It Shows

Write The author repeats the phrase "under the bed" to show that Chip _____

_____

_____

QUICK TIP

When I **reread**, I use the authors words and phrases to help me understand what the characters do.

? How do the poet and authors of *A Window Into History: The Mystery of the Cellar Window* and "A Second Chance for Chip: The Case of the Curious Canine" help you see the benefits of taking a second look?

QUICK TIP
The poet helps me understand how important a second look is. I can compare text to poetry.

Talk About It Read the poem. Talk with a partner about what the speaker does at the beginning of the poem and what he does at the end.

Cite Text Evidence Work with a partner to circle ways the arrow and the song are similar. Underline ways they are different. Then go back and make a mark in the margin beside the lines that show how the speaker realizes that taking a second look is a good thing to do.

Write When they keep looking, the poet and the characters in the texts discover _____

_____

_____

_____

The Arrow and the Song

I shot an arrow into the air,
It fell to earth, I knew not where;
For, so swiftly it flew, the sight
Could not follow it in its flight.

I breathed a song into the air,
It fell to earth, I knew not where;
For who has sight so keen and strong,
That it can follow the flight of song?

—Henry Wadsworth Longfellow

Rosa

 How does the author help you visualize what Rosa was like?

Literature Anthology:
pages 298–313

Talk About It Reread the last paragraph on page 301. Turn to your partner and talk about what Rosa does when she sits down on the bus.

Cite Text Evidence What words and phrases help describe what Rosa was like? Write text evidence in the chart.

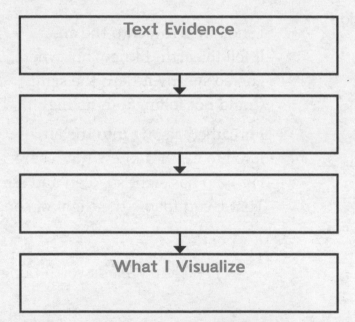

Text Evidence
↓
↓
↓
What I Visualize

Write The author helps me understand what Rosa was like by _____

_____

©OJO Images Ltd/Alamy

Tip of the Week

When I **reread**, I can use the author's words and phrases to visualize what the characters are like. I look for text evidence to answer questions.

Brandon

? **How do you know what Rosa thinks and how she feels as she sits on the bus waiting for the police?**

Talk About It Reread page 304. Turn to a partner and talk about what Rosa thinks about on the bus.

Cite Text Evidence What words and phrases help you know what Rosa is thinking and feeling? Write text evidence in the chart.

What Rosa Thinks	What It Shows

Write I know what Rosa is thinking and feeling on the bus because the author

_____

_____

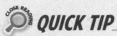 **QUICK TIP**

I can use these sentence frames when we talk about how Rosa feels.

The author tells me that Rosa is thinking about . . .

This helps me understand that she is . . .

Why does the author use Martin Luther King, Jr.'s quote?

 QUICK TIP

When I **reread**, I can use details to help me understand a historical event.

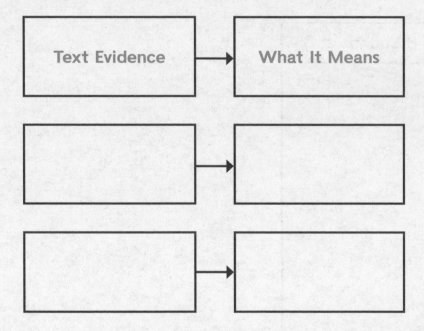

Talk About It Reread the last paragraph on page 308. Turn to a partner and talk about what Martin Luther King, Jr. said.

Cite Text Evidence What does Martin Luther King, Jr.'s quote mean? Cite text evidence and tell why the author includes it in the selection.

Text Evidence		What It Means
	→	
	→	
	→	

Write The author uses Martin Luther King, Jr.'s quote to help me understand

_____

_____

_____

Your Turn

How does Nikki Giovanni use figurative language to help you understand the theme, or message, of this selection? Use these sentence frames to organize your ideas.

Nikki Giovanni's description of Rosa helps me . . .

She also uses similes to . . .

This helps me understand her message by . . .

Go Digital!
Write your response online.

Our Voices, Our Votes

Rights for African Americans

1   During the early 1800s, many women's groups joined with abolitionists to demand equal rights. Abolitionists were people who wanted to end slavery. They believed that freedom was a natural right. Women marched with them in protest. Some of them helped enslaved people escape to places where they could be free. Over 300 people gathered at a convention in Seneca Falls, New York in 1848. They discussed how women's rights were linked to other social and civil rights movements. Some speakers urged that suffrage, or voting rights, be a top priority for African Americans and women.

2   After the Civil War, the United States government added the Thirteenth Amendment, outlawing slavery. Three years later, the Fourteenth Amendment granted former slaves rights as citizens. Finally, in 1870, the Fifteenth Amendment gave male citizens of all races the right to vote. Though many women supported these causes, women still could not vote. Their fight was far from over.

Reread and use the prompts to take notes in the text.

Circle the sentence in the first paragraph that helps you understand who abolitionists were.

Then underline the sentence that explains how the abolitionists and women who wanted suffrage were alike.

COLLABORATE

Reread paragraph 2. Talk with a partner about how the author organizes information. Write numbers in the margin to indicate the order of how laws changed.

Women's Suffrage

3   Women continued to fight for suffrage on the national, state, and local levels. Some were outraged enough to defy voting laws and attempt to cast ballots in elections. These acts of civil disobedience resulted in fines. In some cases, the women ended up in jail.

4   Women's suffrage remained unpopular with many men. Even so, the idea took hold in some areas. In 1869, Wyoming became the first state to allow women to vote in its elections. Over the next twenty years, four more states would grant women this right.

5   Women began to join forces, borrowing ideas from women's groups in other countries. Some hired lobbyists, or people who tried to convince politicians to vote a certain way. Others held huge rallies to raise awareness. Petitions bearing thousands of signatures demanded that the country's laws be amended.

6   President Woodrow Wilson finally agreed that a true democracy should not deny women the right to vote. With his support, Congress drafted the Nineteenth Amendment to the Constitution. In 1920, it was approved.

How do you know that suffrage was an important issue for women? Underline the clue in paragraph 1 that helps you understand how big of a struggle it was.

Reread paragraph 5. Circle the ways women took action. Write them here:

1. _____

2. _____

3. _____

4. _____

COLLABORATE

Talk with a partner about how President Woodrow Wilson influenced how women got the right to vote. Draw a box around the text evidence to support your discussion.

Why is "Our Voices, Our Votes" a good title for this selection?

 **QUICK TIP**

When I **reread**, I can find text evidence to support the selection's title.

Talk About It Reread paragraph 5 on page 118. Talk with a partner about how women joined forces to make changes in the law.

Cite Text Evidence What words and phrases help you understand how women worked together to change the voting laws? Write text evidence in the chart.

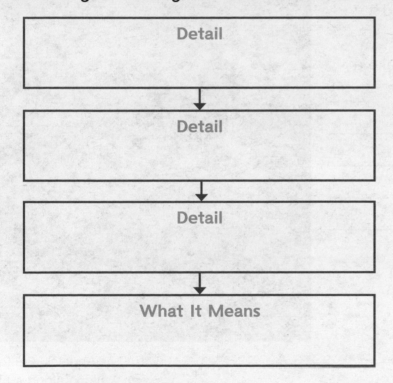

Detail

↓

Detail

↓

Detail

↓

What It Means

Write "Our Voices, Our Votes" is a good title for this selection because _____

_____

_____

? How does the photographer show how the men are taking a stand in the same way the authors of *Rosa* and "Our Voices, Our Votes" show how people have taken a stand?

COLLABORATE

Talk About It Look at the photograph. Read the caption. Talk with a partner about what the two men are doing. Discuss what you see on the billboard.

Cite Text Evidence Circle how the men are taking a stand. Underline what they are taking a stand against.

Write The photographer and authors show how people take a stand by _____

_____

_____

_____

_____

Library of Congress Prints and Photographs Division [LC-USZC4-8174]

QUICK TIP

I can use details in the photograph to help me compare it to text.

"Toward Los Angeles, California" shows two men walking along a highway. The photograph was taken in 1937.

One Well

Literature Anthology:
pages 320–335

? How does the author help you understand the water cycle by using a diagram to show that all the water on Earth comes from just one well?

COLLABORATE

Talk About It Reread page 324. Look at the diagram. Turn to your partner and talk about what the diagram shows.

Cite Text Evidence What clues from the text and diagram show that all water on Earth comes from one well? Write text evidence in the chart.

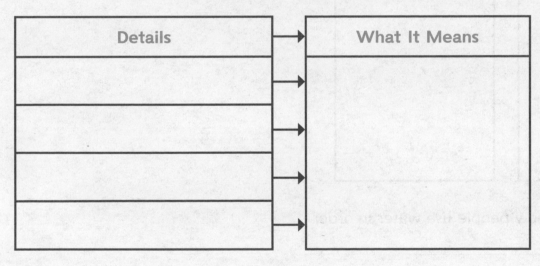

Details		What It Means
	→	
	→	
	→	
	→	

Write The text and the diagram helps me understand the author's point by

_____

_____

CLOSE READING

Tip of the Week

When I **reread**, I can use diagrams to help me understand the information. I look for text evidence to answer questions.

Natalie

Mark Bowden/iStock/360/Getty Images

? **Why does the author include captions that describe how people use water?**

COLLABORATE

Talk About It Reread the captions on page 331. Talk to a partner about what the captions tell you.

Cite Text Evidence What clues in the captions help you see how people use water? Write text evidence in the chart and tell why the author uses them.

Captions	Illustrations	Author's Purpose

Write The author includes captions describing how people use water in order to _____

_____

_____

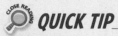
QUICK TIP

I can use these sentence frames when we talk about how people use water.

The author uses illustrations and captions to . . .

The author includes them to help me . . .

? **Why is "Saving the Water in the Well" a good heading for the last part of the selection?**

COLLABORATE

Talk About It Reread the third paragraph on page 334. Turn to a partner and talk about conserving water.

Cite Text Evidence What words and phrases help show that conserving water is important? Write text evidence in the chart.

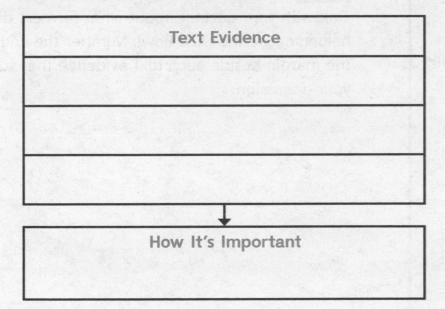

Text Evidence

↓

How It's Important

Write "Saving the Water in the Well" is a good heading because _____

_____

_____

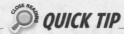

QUICK TIP

When I **reread**, I can use text evidence to understand what the author wants me to know.

Your Turn

How does the author's use of text features support her message that water is valuable? Use these sentence frames to organize your text evidence.

The author uses diagrams to . . .

The headings help me understand that . . .

This supports her message because . . .

Go Digital!
Write your response online.

The Dirt on Dirt

[1]   In the 1930s, a drought struck the Great Plains, the central region of the United States. This area once was covered with tall grasses that anchored the soil. Over the years, farmers had cut these grasses and planted crops. The land was planted with the same crops year after year and the soil was not given a chance to restore its nutrients. By the time the drought struck, the soil was worn out. Soon the soil began to blow away in huge black clouds. These dust storms devastated the land, sending farmers and their families elsewhere. This area became known as the Dust Bowl.

[2]   Why did this happen? Soil helps store and move nutrients and water through the earth. Without these, soil cannot provide a habitat for other living things. The dust storms of the 1930s made people realize that healthy soil is a necessity.

Reread and use the prompts to take notes in the text.

Underline the sentence in paragraph 1 that explains the effect that the dust storms had on farms. Circle what the farmers had to do.

COLLABORATE

Talk with your partner about what farmers did that helped cause the Dust Bowl. Number the causes in the margin beside each text evidence that supports your discussion.

Siede Preis/Photodisc/Getty Images

Gaining Ground

[1]   People today are more aware of the importance of soil then they were in the 1930s so they have taken steps to conserve and protect it. Although current practices like the use of pesticides on crops can still pollute groundwater and harm organisms in the soil, governments and industries are working to develop safer chemicals. Many farmers take steps to keep soil healthy by alternating crops so soil nutrients are not used up. Others also plant trees as barriers that will keep the wind from blowing the soil away. The work of all these people keep the soil safe, full of nutrients, and, most importantly, in place.

Siede Preis/Photodisc/Getty Images

Circle the phrase in the excerpt that shows that some farmers are still polluting the ground. Then underline the sentence that tells what is being done to change that.

COLLABORATE

Talk with a partner about how the use of pesticides affects the soil. Make marks in the margin beside the text evidence to support this. Write it here:

1. _____

2. _____

Now draw a box around the things that are being done by farmers to keep soil healthy.

? How does the author help you understand how people are working to keep the soil safe?

COLLABORATE

Talk About It Reread the excerpt on page 124. Talk with a partner about what people are doing to keep the soil safe.

Cite Text Evidence What phrases tell about what farmers are doing to protect the soil? Write text evidence in the chart.

Text Evidence	What I Understand

Write I see how people are working to keep the soil safe because the author

_____

_____

_____

QUICK TIP

When I reread, I can use the author's words and phrases to help me understand the topic.

Siede Preis/Photodisc/Getty Images

What does the mural have to say about natural resources that is also conveyed in *One Well* and "The Dirt on Dirt"?

John Flournoy/McGraw-Hill Education

COLLABORATE

Talk About It With a partner, discuss the mural. Talk about the natural resources that you see. What is being done with the natural resources?

Cite Text Evidence Look at the mural. Work with a partner to circle the natural resources that are pictured. Make notes in the margin that tell what is being done with them.

Write The mural and the two selections convey the ideas that _____

_____

_____

_____

_____

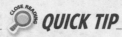

QUICK TIP

I see how natural resources are used in the mural. This will help me compare it to the selections I read this week.

This mural is part of a larger mural painted along a street in San Francisco, California.

Words as Confetti

? How does the poet's use of free verse create the poem's mood?

Literature Anthology:
pages 340–342

COLLABORATE

Talk About It Reread page 340 out loud with a partner. Talk about how the poem makes you feel.

Cite Text Evidence What words and phrases does the poet use to create mood? Write text evidence in the chart below.

Text Evidence	How It Creates Mood

Write The poet uses free verse to create the poem's mood by _____

_____

CLOSE READING **Tip** of the **Week**

When I **reread**, I can think about how the poet uses structure to create mood. I look for text evidence to answer questions.

Esther

Lane Oatey/Blue Jean Images/Getty Images

Dreams

? In "Dreams," how does the poet use repetition and meter to help you understand his message?

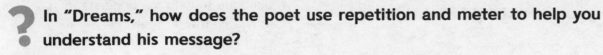

Talk About It Reread page 342. Turn to your partner and discuss what you notice about the way the poem is organized and how that relates to the theme.

Cite Text Evidence What phrases are repeated and how do they help the poet share his message? Write text evidence in the chart.

Text Evidence	Organization	Effect on Reader

Write The poet uses repetition and meter to _____

_____

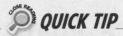 **QUICK TIP**

When I reread, I can use how the poet repeats phrases to help share his message.

Your Turn

How do the poets use repetition and meter to help convey the theme of their poems? Use these sentence frames to organize your text evidence.

In her poem, Pat Mora . . .

Langston Hughes uses repetition to . . .

This helps me understand the poets' messages because . . .

Go Digital!
Write your response online.

A Story of How a Wall Stands

 How does the poet use dialogue to help you understand how his father feels about his work?

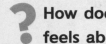

Talk About It Reread page 344. Talk with a partner about how the poet's father describes how he built a wall.

Cite Text Evidence What words and phrases help you figure out how the father feels about his work? Write evidence in the chart.

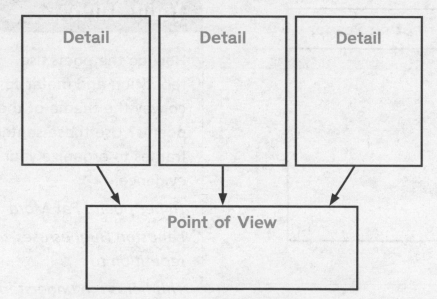

Detail

Detail

Detail

Point of View

Write The poet uses dialogue to show that his father feels _____

_____

_____

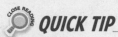 **QUICK TIP**

When I reread, I can use dialogue to help me understand how a character feels.

? How does the poet help you see his point of view about his father?

COLLABORATE

Talk About It Reread the last stanza on page 345. With a partner, discuss how the poet feels about his father's work.

Cite Text Evidence What words in the dialogue show how the poet feels about his father's work? Write text evidence in the chart.

Building a Wall

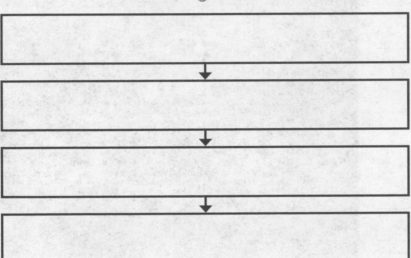

Write The poet uses dialogue to help me understand his point of view by _____

_____

_____

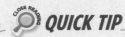
QUICK TIP

Memorize the first stanza on page 345. Recite it to a partner as if you are telling the story of how a wall stands. I can use the poet's words to help me understand how he feels.

Sascha/Photodisc/Getty Images

? How do the sculptors of this statue convey how they feel in the same way the poets use words to express feelings in "Words Free as Confetti" and "A Story of How a Wall Stands"?

Carol M. Highsmith's America, Library of Congress, Prints and Photographs Division.

QUICK TIP

I can use details in the sculpture to help me compare art to poetry.

COLLABORATE

Talk About It Look at the photograph. Read the caption. With a partner, talk about how the sculptors conveyed their feelings through art.

Cite Text Evidence Circle details in the photograph that tell you something about Abraham Lincoln. Underline clues that show the message the sculptors wanted to express.

Write The sculptors and poets convey how they feel by _____

_____

_____

_____

_____

_____

This bronze statue depicts Abraham Lincoln and his horse, Old Bob, at the Lincoln Summer Home in Washington, D.C. It was created in 2009 by Ivan Schwartz, Stuart Williamson, and Jiwoong Cheh.

Ida B. . .and Her Plans to Maximize Fun, Avoid Disaster, and (Possibly) Save the World

Literature Anthology:
pages 346–357

? What does Ida's impression of the other students tell you about her?

COLLABORATE

Talk About It Reread the last paragraph on page 349. Turn to your partner and discuss why Ida thinks the other students are agreeing with Ms. W. so enthusiastically.

Cite Text Evidence What does Ida's perception about her fellow students help you understand about her? Write and explain text evidence in the chart.

Tip of the Week

When I **reread**, I can think about what characters' thoughts and actions tell me about them. I look for text evidence to answer questions.

What the other students are doing

↓

Why Ida thinks the students are doing this

↓

What Ida's impression tells the reader about her

Gilbert

Write Ida's impression of the other students shows _____

_____

Ana Abejon/iStock/360/Getty Images

How does the author help you understand Ida's reaction to reading to the class?

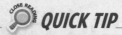**QUICK TIP**

I can use these sentence frames when we talk about how characters change.

When Ida started at her new school, she wanted to be . . .

After reading to her class, she feels . . .

COLLABORATE

Talk About It Reread the last three paragraphs on page 353. Turn to your partner and discuss what happened and how they make Ida feel.

Cite Text Evidence What words and phrases show how Ida changes? Write text evidence and explain how she reacts to that change.

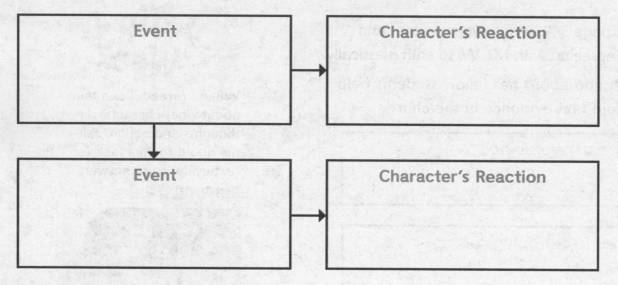

| Event | Character's Reaction |

| Event | Character's Reaction |

Write The author helps me understand Ida's reaction to reading by _____

_____

_____

_____

? **How does the author help you understand how Ida B feels?**

Talk About It Reread page 357. Turn to a partner and talk about Ida B's mood.

Cite Text Evidence What words and phrases help you understand Ida B's mood? Use text evidence in your answer.

Text Evidence	How It Helps

Write I understand how Ida B feels because the author _____

_____

_____

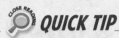

QUICK TIP

When I **reread**, I can think about how the author uses words and phrases to reveal a character's mood.

Your Turn

The author includes many details in the story to help characterize Ida B. How do these details show how Ida B changes between the beginning and the end of the story? Use these sentence frames to organize your text evidence.

At the beginning, the author describes Ida B . . .

The author reveals a change in Ida's character by . . .

At the end, the author's details show that Ida B is . . .

Go Digital!
Write your response online.

A Dusty Ride

1 Outside, Ravi wondered, *Explore what?* Although he'd been there several weeks, he hadn't seen anything worth exploring. Then he remembered the dirt path he saw earlier and headed toward the side of the house.

2 Ravi had not gotten far down the path when he heard the hedgerow nearby rustle. As the shrubs began to shake, he detected heavy breathing and what sounded like a snort. Picturing a gigantic beast on the other side, Ravi retreated but then paused at the sound of a voice. He turned to see a woman on horseback emerge from the shrubs.

3 Seeing Ravi, the woman pulled the reins, stopping the horse in its tracks. He'd never seen a horse up close, and from his perspective, it was a towering giant.

Reread and use the prompts to take notes in the text.

Underline the words that explain why the horse seemed like a towering giant to Ravi. Write why the author includes this detail.

_____

_____

_____

Talk with your partner about why Ravi does not like living in the country.

4   "Hi!" the woman said, dismounting. "I hope we didn't scare you. I'm Lila, this is Dusty, and we live at the farm down the road. I was just coming by to welcome you!"

5   Sensing Ravi's hesitation, Lila exclaimed, "No need to be scared of this old guy. In fact, Dusty is rather unique because he seems to sense your feelings: If you're scared, he gets nervous, but if you're calm, he's as cool as a cucumber." She gave him a wink, and added, "But Dusty has a way of calming people."

6   Ravi's parents came outside upon hearing Lila's voice, and, as the three introduced themselves, Ravi eyed the horse uneasily and noticed that the horse seemed to eye him, too.

Reread paragraph 5. Circle the sentences in which Lila explains how Dusty reacts to people. Write them here:

_____

_____

COLLABORATE

Reread paragraphs 4 and 5. Talk about what Lila says when she stops by Ravi's house.

In paragraph 6, draw a box around what happens between Ravi and Dusty. How does this confirm what Lila said about Dusty earlier?

_____

_____

Why is "A Dusty Ride" a good title for this story?

Talk About It Reread the excerpts on pages 136–137. With a partner, talk about how the word *dusty* is important to the story.

Cite Text Evidence What could the word *dusty* in the title mean? Write text evidence in the chart.

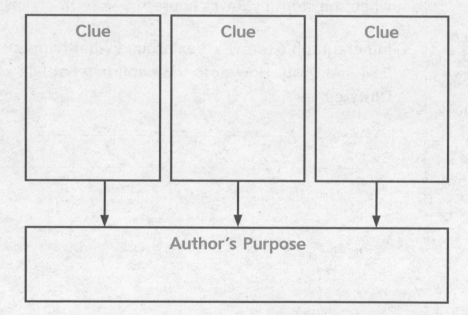

Write "A Dusty Ride" is a good title for this story because _____

_____

_____

_____

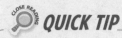 **QUICK TIP**

When I **reread**, I will pay close attention to how the mood changes in a story.

How does the artist show Edma and Jeanne's relationship in the painting and how is it similar to the way the authors describe the families in *Ida B*... and "A Dusty Ride"?

Image courtesy National Gallery of Art

COLLABORATE

Talk About It Talk with a partner about the painting. Read the caption. Talk about what you see and how it makes you feel.

Cite Text Evidence Circle details in the painting that help you understand the relationship between Edma and Jeanne. Think about the relationships you read about this week.

Write The artist and authors describe relationships by _____

_____

_____

_____

_____

_____

_____

The Artist's Sister, Edma, with Her Daughter, Jeanne is a watercolor that was painted in 1872 by French artist Berthe Morisot.

Bud, Not Buddy

? What does the author reveal about Bud through his responses to the conversation he overhears?

Literature Anthology: pages 364–377

Talk About It Reread page 366. Turn to your partner and discuss what Bud thinks and does. Discuss why he reacts in this way.

Cite Text Evidence What does Bud do after he overhears the conversation? Write text evidence in the chart.

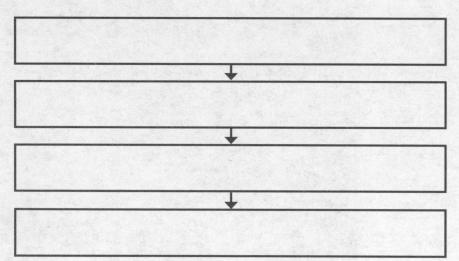

Write The author helps me know more about Bud by _____

_____

Tip of the **Week**

When I **reread**, I can think about what motivates characters. I look for text evidence to answer questions.

Bree

Emma Kim/Cultura RF/Getty Images

How does the author show how Bud will have to change to stay with the band?

Talk About It Reread page 370. Turn to your partner and discuss what Bud is expected to do.

Cite Text Evidence How is what Bud is expected to do different from what he is used to? Write text evidence in the chart.

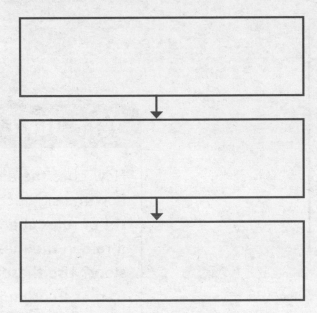

Write The author helps me understand how Bud will have to change by _____

_____

_____

QUICK TIP

I can use these sentence frames when we talk about how Bud will have to change.

Bud used to . . .

Now Bud will have to . . .

? **How does the author help you understand how Bud changes as he becomes part of the band?**

COLLABORATE

Talk About It Reread page 376. Turn to a partner and discuss how Bud feels about his new nickname and what he is expected to do.

Cite Text Evidence What words and phrases help you see how Bud changes? Write text evidence.

Text Evidence	How It Helps

Write I understand how Bud changes because the author _____

_____

_____

QUICK TIP

When I reread, I can think about why characters act a certain way.

Your Turn

How does the author show how the significance of Bud's set of rules changes and plays a role in the message of the story? Use these sentence frames to organize your text evidence.

The rules change . . .

This is important because . . .

This affects the story . . .

Go Digital!
Write your response online.

Musical Impressions of the Great Depression

Sympathy through Song

1   Many songs of the 1930s, particularly in folk and country music, recounted people's stories of loss and hardship. The songwriter Woody Guthrie followed farm workers who traveled west to California hoping to find work. He saw that they often encountered new and tougher challenges. Guthrie expressed sympathy for them through songs like "Dust Bowl Blues" and "Goin' Down the Road Feeling Bad." He hoped to restore people's sense of dignity.

2   Meanwhile, across the country, the Carter Family performed similar songs, such as "Worried Man Blues," describing life in the Appalachian Mountains where resources were scarce. Listeners found comfort in the knowledge that they were not alone in their struggles.

Reread and use the prompts to take notes in the text.

Reread the excerpt. Underline the sentence that explains the goal of Woody Guthrie's music. Write how this kind of music affected people who struggled during this time.

_____

_____

_____

COLLABORATE

Talk with your partner about why music was able to change how people felt during a difficult time. Underline text evidence in the excerpt.

On the Up-Swing

3   Times were certainly hard in the country. In the nation's cities, the situation was equally difficult. In some African-American communities, unemployment soared above fifty percent. These challenges reminded some of earlier times of slavery, and many found comfort in the musical styles of that era: gospel and blues.

4   Jazz, a newer form of music with upbeat rhythms, lifted people's spirits. Band leaders like Duke Ellington and Count Basie created a new, high-energy style of jazz called swing. Around the country, people of all races responded to these positive rhythms. People left their problems behind and escaped onto the dance floor.

5   In New York, Broadway musicals delighted theatergoers. Many musicals offered light entertainment, while others addressed the current hardships through songs, such as "Brother, Can You Spare a Dime?"

Reread paragraphs 3 and 4. Circle examples of music that was affecting people.

COLLABORATE

With a partner, talk about how the author describes the different kinds of music.

Underline a sentence in paragraph 5 that describes another kind of music that affected people.

Why is "On the Up-Swing" a good heading for this section? Use text evidence to support your answer.

_____

_____

_____

? **What is the author's purpose for writing this selection?**

Talk About It Reread the excerpts. Talk with a partner about what the author wants you to know about music during the Great Depression.

Cite Text Evidence What words and phrases tell you why the author wrote this selection? Write text evidence in the chart.

Clues	Author's Purpose

Write The author's purpose for writing this selection was _____

_____

_____

_____

QUICK TIP

When I reread, I will pay close attention to the details that the author provides.

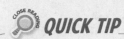

How do this photograph and the selections *Bud, Not Buddy* and "Musical Impressions of the Great Depression" demonstrate the effects that music can have on people?

COLLABORATE

Talk About It Look at the photograph. Read the caption. With a partner, talk about what is going on and how it makes you feel.

Cite Text Evidence Circle details in the photograph that help you understand what people are feeling. Draw a box around the main focus of the photo.

Write The photograph and selections show _____

_____

_____

_____

_____

_____

QUICK TIP

I see how music affects people in the photograph. This will help me compare it to the selections I read this week.

William P. Gottlieb/Ira and Leonore S. Gershwin Fund Collection, Music Division, Library of Congress

Portrait of Ella Fitzgerald with Dizzy Gillespie, Ray Brown, and other musicians at the Downbeat Club in New York in 1947.

Global Warming

Literature Anthology:
pages 384–397

? Why does the author begin the selection with a photograph of the Earth from outer space?

COLLABORATE

Talk About It Look at the photograph on pages 384–385. Turn to your partner and discuss what you see.

Cite Text Evidence What clues in the photograph help you see what the author wants you to understand about Earth? Write clues in the chart.

Author's Purpose

CLOSE READING **Tip** of the **Week**

When I **reread**, I can use photographs to help me understand information. I look for text evidence to answer questions.

Jane

Write The author uses the photograph at the beginning of the selection to _____

_____

_____

_____

kristian sekulic/iStock/360/Getty Images

? How does the author use photographs to help you understand climate change?

Talk About It Analyze the photographs on page 391. Talk with a partner about how they are different and what the author was trying to convey by using them.

Cite Visual Evidence What clues in the photographs help you understand climate change? Write clues in the chart.

Photograph Clues: 1957	Photograph Clues: 2004

Write The author uses photographs to help me understand _____

_____

_____

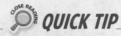
I can use these sentence frames when we talk about climate change.

The difference between the photographs is . . .

They help me understand . . .

? **Why does the author end the selection with a photograph of a young plant?**

COLLABORATE

Talk About It Reread the last two paragraphs on page 397. Look at the photograph. Turn to a partner and discuss what the photograph shows.

Cite Visual Evidence What words and phrases in the text help you understand why the author uses the photograph? Write clues in the chart.

Text Evidence	Author's Purpose

Write The author ends the selection with a photograph of a young plant to

_____

_____

_____

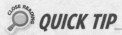
QUICK TIP
I can think about why the author includes photographs in a text.

Your Turn

How do the photographs in this selection help you understand how living things are affected by climate change? Use these sentence frames to organize your text evidence.

The author uses photographs that show . . .

The photographs are important because . . .

This helps me understand . . .

Go Digital!
Write your response online.

When Volcanoes Erupt

1   On the morning of May 18, 1980, gray ash drifted from the sky near Mount Saint Helens, Washington, turning day into night. A volcano had erupted, sending an ash cloud thousands of feet into the sky. Rock debris and ice fell from the mountain and was pushed by the eruption across nearby lakes and ridges. The eruption went on for just nine hours, but in that time the surrounding landscape completely changed.

Vents in the Earth

2   What causes a volcano like Mount Saint Helens to erupt? Beneath Earth's rocky crust, there is a layer that consists partly of hot, melted rock. This molten rock is called magma. A gradual buildup of pressure caused by gases within Earth can cause magma to burst or seep through vents, or opening, in Earth's surface.

Reread and use the prompts to take notes in the text.

Reread paragraph 1. Draw a box around the words that show the visual impact of the volcanic eruption.

COLLABORATE

Reread paragraph 2. Talk with a partner about what causes a volcanic eruption. Underline text evidence to support your discussion.

Why is "Vents in the Earth" a good heading for this section? Use text evidence.

_____

_____

_____

_____

_____

The Impact of Volcanoes

1   There are about 50 volcanic eruptions that occur somewhere in the world every year. Many are concentrated in an area of the Pacific Ocean known as the "Ring of Fire." The most frequent volcanoes in the United States occur in Hawaii and in the southwestern island chain off of Alaska. Volcanoes in the Cascade Range, the mountain range that runs from western Canada south through California, are less frequent but can be more dangerous.

2   Eruptions can devastate surrounding areas. An eruption can spew lava, ash, rocks, mud, and poisonous gases in to the air and harm nearby plants, animals, and people. Crops and property can be destroyed.

In paragraph 1, underline words and phrases that tell where volcanoes erupt most frequently.

COLLABORATE

Reread paragraph 2. With a partner, discuss the immediate effects that an eruption has on the landscape around the volcano. Circle text evidence that supports your discussion.

How does the author help you understand the effects of a volcanic eruption? Use text evidence to help support your response.

_____

_____

_____

_____

Why does the author use vivid language to describe volcanic eruptions?

Talk About It Reread the excerpts on pages 150 and 151. Talk with a partner about how vivid language helps you visualize volcanic eruptions.

Cite Text Evidence What words and phrases help you picture what volcanic eruptions are like? Write text evidence.

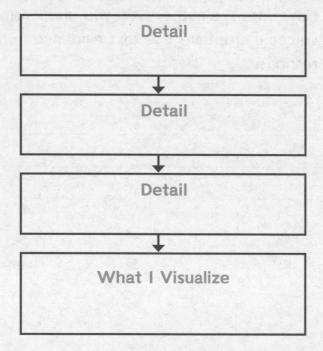

Detail

↓

Detail

↓

Detail

↓

What I Visualize

Write The author uses vivid language to describe volcanic eruptions _____

_____

_____

_____

 **QUICK TIP**

When I reread, I can use words and phrases to help me visualize information.

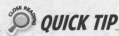

QUICK TIP

I can use words and phrases to compare the poem to the selections I read this week.

? How does Walt Whitman capture the strength of nature that is discussed in *Global Warming* and "When Volcanoes Erupt"?

COLLABORATE

Talk About It With a partner, discuss the poem. Talk about how Walt Whitman describes nature.

Cite Text Evidence Circle words and phrases that describe the storm. Underline details that help you understand how the storm sounds.

Write The poet captures the strength of nature like in *Global Warming* and "When Volcanoes Erupt" _____

_____

_____

_____

_____

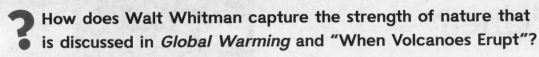

Proud Music of the Storm!

Blast that careers so free,
whistling across the prairies!

Strong hum of forest tree-tops!
Wind of the mountains!

Personified dim shapes!
you hidden orchestras!

You serenades of phantoms,
with instruments alert,

Blending, with Nature's rhythms,
all the tongues of nations. . .

—Walt Whitman
(from *Leaves of Grass*, first published in 1871 72 edition)

Comstock/Stockbyte/Getty Images

When Is a Planet Not a Planet?

? How does the author use the first part of "Pluto's Problems" to support her ideas about Pluto?

Literature Anthology: pages 404–419

COLLABORATE

Talk About It Reread page 407. Turn to a partner and discuss how the information in the section relates to the heading.

Cite Text Evidence What information does the author want you to know about Pluto? Write text evidence in the chart.

Alike: Planets	Different: Pluto

Write The author supports her ideas in "Pluto's Problems" by _____

_____

_____

CLOSE READING **Tip** of the **Week**

When I **reread**, I can think about how the author organizes information. I can find text evidence to answer questions.

April

Leland Bobbe/Photodisc/Getty Images

How does the author use diagrams to help you understand more about the solar system?

Talk About It Reread the diagram and caption on page 410. Turn to your partner and discuss how the diagram connects to the main text.

Cite Text Evidence How does including the diagram support the ideas the author is developing? Cite text evidence from the diagram.

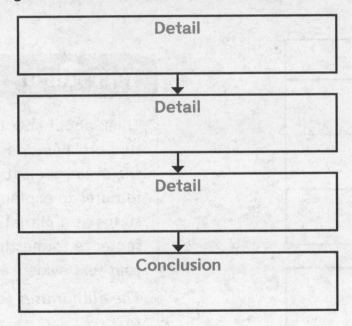

Write The author uses the solar system diagram to help me understand _____

_____

_____

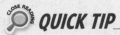
QUICK TIP

I can use these sentence frames when we talk about the diagram.

The diagram helps me see . . .

I know that Pluto . . .

? How does the author use the description of a schoolyard bully to help you understand what she means by the phrase "clearing the neighborhood"?

COLLABORATE

Talk About It Reread page 416. Turn to a partner and talk about what "clearing the neighborhood" means.

Cite Text Evidence What words and phrases tell how some planets are like schoolyard bullies? Write text evidence in the chart.

Text Evidence

↓

Author's Purpose

Write The author's description of a schoolyard bully helps me to understand how planets _____

_____

_____

QUICK TIP
When I reread, I can use how the author makes comparisons to help me understand scientific concepts.

Your Turn

Think about how the author supports her ideas. How does she use organization and text features to explain Pluto's status as a planet? Use these sentence frames to organize your text evidence.

The author uses text features to . . .

She organizes information to . . .

The way she supports her ideas helps me to . . .

Go Digital!
Write your response online.

New Moon

1   On July 20, 2069, a team of four students and their professor leave Earth, heading for the Moon to study its composition.

2   "We are approximately 300 kilometers from the surface of the Moon. Prepare for lunar landing."

3   "Wait! Hold this course! I am getting another reading—there appears to be another object just beyond the Moon."

4   "Based on its movements, it seems to be held in orbit by Earth's gravitational pull."

5   "What could it be?"

6   "Hmmm...if we know the distances between the object, the Moon, and our ship, we should be able to calculate the object's diameter and mass. Then we can run this data through the supercomputer and compare it against information about all known objects in our solar system."

Reread and use the prompts to take notes in the text.

Reread paragraph 1. Circle the phrase that tells when this story takes place, who is traveling, and where they are going.

COLLABORATE

Reread the dialogue. Talk with your partner about how it helps you understand more about the events in the story.

Underline details that tell you what problem the group encounters. Write details on these lines.

_____

_____

_____

_____

1   "How can that be?"

2   "Unlike Earth, Mars has two moons. A strong force would have had to knock one of Mars's moons out of orbit—another object might have collided with it!"

3   "Like an asteroid?"

4   "Precisely."

5   "Look! We are approaching the moon from Mars!"

6   BEEP! BEEP!

7   "I'm getting emergency messages from Earth! The tides are rising rapidly!"

8   "Rising tides? I bet this moon from Mars is the cause!"

9   "That's right, Luis. The Moon affects tides on Earth. A new object entering Earth's orbit would change the gravitational pull between the Earth and the Moon and alter the tides."

10   "What do we do?"

11   "We need to force this moon back into Mars's gravitational field before there is a real disaster. Mark, fire up the Asteroid Simulator Beam!"

Reread the excerpt. Circle the sentence that describes a problem on Earth.

Underline words and phrases that show the students' solution to the problem.

With a partner, talk about the problem that the students encounter while in space. How does what the character says help you understand how the characters deal with the problem?

Make a mark in the margin beside text evidence that supports your answer.

? How does the author help you understand his purpose for writing this story?

COLLABORATE

Talk About It Reread the excerpt on page 158. With a partner, talk about what happens.

Cite Text Evidence What words and phrases help you know why the author wrote this story? Write them here and tell the author's purpose.

Text Evidence	Author's Purpose

Write The author's purpose for writing this story is _____

_____

_____

_____

? How do the way the artist and the authors of *When is a Planet Not a Planet?* and "New Moon" help you understand how scientific knowledge changes over time?

COLLABORATE

Talk About It Look at the painting. Read the caption. Talk with a partner about what you see in the painting.

Cite Text Evidence Circle what the artist wants you to focus on. Think about how the knowledge about our solar system has changed over time. Reread the caption and underline evidence that helps you understand how a comet inspired scientific knowledge.

Write The artist and authors show how knowledge changes

over time by _____

_____

_____

_____

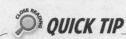

QUICK TIP

I see a rare comet in the painting. This will help me compare it to the selections I I read this week.

Digital Image: Yale Center for British Art

Giovanni Battista Donati discovered this comet over Florence, Italy on June 2, 1858. It was observed and studied by many astronomers. The comet became the subject of newspaper and magazine articles. William Turner's painting captures the comet's curved tail. Donati's comet inspired many scientists and people to learn more about the night sky.

The Case of the Missing Bees

*Literature Anthology:
pages 424–427*

? Why does the author begin the selection with a question?

Talk About It Reread the first paragraph on page 425. Talk with a partner about what the question helps you understand about bees.

Cite Text Evidence How does the author organize the first paragraph? Write text evidence in the chart.

Clues

↓

Author's Purpose

Write The author begins the article with a question to _____

_____

_____

Tip of the Week

When I **reread**, I will think about how the author structures the text. I look for text evidence to answer questions.

Vince

laflor/iStock/360/Getty Images

? How does the author's use of headings help you understand his point of view about pesticides?

COLLABORATE

Talk About It Look at the headings on pages 426–427. Turn to a partner and discuss how the headings help the author tell how he feels about pesticides.

Cite Text Evidence What words and phrases support the author's headings? Write text evidence and tell how it shows his point of view.

The Unusual Suspects	Are Pesticides to Blame?	Author's Point of View

Write The author uses headings to _____

_____

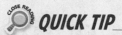

Your Turn

Think about how each persuasive article is organized. Which author's style is more convincing and why? Use these sentence frames to organize text evidence.

The author of "A Germ of an Idea" thinks . . .

The author of "Pointing to Pesticides" believes . . .

The way the authors organize information helps me see that . . .

Go Digital!
Write your response online.

Busy, Beneficial Bees

1 In the U.S., honeybees pollinate about $15 billion worth of crops a year. That's on top of the $150 million worth of honey they produce annually. Although some crops can be pollinated by other nectar-feeding insects, many crops depend specifically on honeybees for pollination. Without honeybees, our crops and our economy would really feel the sting!

Crops Depend on Honeybees

Many crops depend on insects to pollinate them. For some crops, honeybees make up a large percentage of those pollinators.

Crop	Dependence on Insect Pollination	Proportion that are Honeybees
Alfalfa, hay & seed	100%	60%
Apples	100%	90%
Almonds	100%	100%
Citrus	20–80%	10–90%
Cotton	20%	90%
Soybeans	10%	50%
Broccoli	100%	90%
Carrots	100%	90%
Cantaloupe	80%	90%

Numbers based on estimates in 2000. Source: Compiled by CRS using values reported in R. A. Morse, and N.W. Calderone, *The Value of Honey Bees as Pollinators of U.S. Crops in 2000*, March 2000, Cornell University.

Reread and use the prompts to take notes in the text.

Reread paragraph 1. Underline how the author feels about honeybees. Write it here:

_____

_____

Reread the section "Crops Depend on Honeybees." Talk with a partner about why the author includes the chart in this selection. Circle text evidence to support your discussion.

Make marks in the table beside the top four crops that depend on insect and honeybee pollination.

? How does the author use a table to help you understand why bees are so important?

COLLABORATE

Talk About It Reread the table on page 163. With a partner, discuss how it helps support the author's point of view about honeybees.

Cite Text Evidence What information in the table helps support the author's point of view about the importance of bees? Write text evidence in the chart.

Evidence	Author's Purpose

Write I understand why bees are so important because the author uses a

table to _____

_____

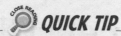 **QUICK TIP**

When I reread, I can use evidence from a table to help me understand the author's point of view.

? How does the poet and the authors of "The Case of the Missing Bees" and "Busy, Beneficial Bees" help you understand their point of view about how humans and animals affect each other?

Daniel Trim Photography/Getty Images

COLLABORATE

Talk About It Read the poem. Talk with a partner about who the poet is speaking to and what his message is.

Cite Text Evidence Circle words and phrases in the poem that tell what the poet asks children not to do. Underline how the poet says the animals will react to kindness. Think about this poet's point of view and how it compares to the points of view of the authors of the selections you read this week.

Write I know how the poet and the authors feel about how humans and

animals interact because _____

_____

_____

_____

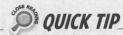

QUICK TIP

I can see how the poet feels about animals. This will help me compare poetry to text.

Kindness to Animals

Little children, never give
Pain to things that feel and live:
Let the gentle robin come
For the crumbs you save at home,—
As his meat you throw along
He'll repay you with a song;
Never hurt the timid hare
Peeping from her green grass lair,
Let her come and sport and play
On the lawn at close of day.

— Anonymous

The Unbreakable Code

? Why does Grandfather speak to John in Navajo?

COLLABORATE

Talk About It Reread pages 432 and 433. Turn to your partner and discuss how the Navajo language is described in the selection.

Cite Text Evidence What effect does the Navajo language have on John? Write text evidence in the web.

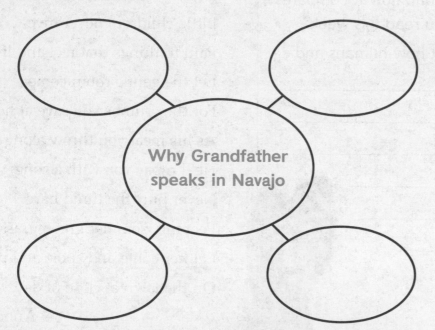

Why Grandfather speaks in Navajo

Write Grandfather speaks to John in Navajo because _____

_____

_____

Literature Anthology:
pages 430–443

CLOSE READING
Tip of the Week

When I **reread**, I can use the author's words and phrases to understand the characters. I find text evidence to answer questions.

Roberto

? **Why was it important to the story that Grandfather's World War II mission was a secret?**

COLLABORATE

Talk About It Reread pages 436 and 437. Turn to your partner and discuss how the Navajo code is set up.

Cite Text Evidence What words and phrases tell about the secrecy of Grandfather's mission? Write text evidence.

Text Evidence

↓

Conclusion

Write It was important to the story that Grandfather's World War II mission

is a secret because _____

_____

QUICK TIP

I can use these sentence frames when we talk about Grandfather's mission.

The author includes many details about . . .

This tells me that . . .

How does John's reaction to his Grandfather's words show how John has changed?

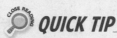 **QUICK TIP**

I can think about how the author uses dialogue to share key details.

COLLABORATE

Talk About It Reread page 443. Turn to a partner and discuss how John has changed by the end of the story.

Cite Text Evidence How does Grandfather's story change the way John feels? Cite evidence from the text in your answer.

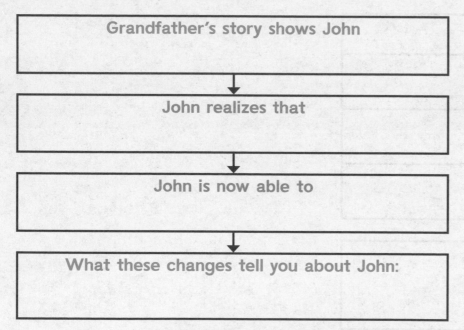

Grandfather's story shows John

↓

John realizes that

↓

John is now able to

↓

What these changes tell you about John:

Write By the end of the story, John _____

_____

_____

Your Turn

How does the author use dialogue and Grandfather's story to teach John about the strengths of his Navajo culture? Use these sentence frames to organize your text evidence.

The author includes Grandfather's stories to . . .

John's reaction to these stories shows that . . .

In the end, John . . .

Go Digital!
Write your response online.

Allies in Action

Joining the Allies

1   Many men left the United States to fight in the war. Women also enlisted, often serving in the Army Nurse Corps. The large number of recruits that went overseas caused a worker shortage back home. In response, many women took jobs previously held by men. They held positions in government and worked in factories. They also raised funds and collected materials that would be recycled into supplies for the troops.

2   The shortage of workers in agriculture led the United States to institute the Bracero Program with Mexico. *Bracero* is the Spanish word for laborer. This program encouraged Mexican workers to offer assistance to farm owners in the United States. These skilled workers helped maintain crops, keeping the country's economy productive during the war.

Reread and use the prompts to take notes in the text.

Underline a sentence in paragraph 1 that explains why help from women was needed.

Talk with a partner about why the United States needed the help of women and people from other countries.

Underline the words in paragraph 2 that explain how the Bracero Program worked. Explain why the author included this information in the text.

_____

_____

_____

_____

The Tuskegee Airmen

3   By the start of the war, a number of African American men were already active in the military. However, their positions were limited. They were rarely given opportunities for advancement and special military operations.

4   Many civil rights groups had protested these restrictions on African Americans. In response, the U.S. Army Air Corps began a new training program in 1941. They taught African Americans how to become pilots and navigators. This program was based in Tuskegee, Alabama. Those who completed aeronautic, or pilot, training there became known as "The Tuskegee Airmen."

5   The Tuskegee Airmen flew many missions during World War II. Over time, they gained a strong reputation for their skills. Their success would lead the U.S. military to recognize African American service and offer them more training opportunities in different fields.

Circle the words that tell you that African Americans did not have the same opportunities as white soldiers.

Draw a box around the sentence that explains what happened as a result.

Reread the excerpt on this page. With a partner, talk about what the text says in reference to African Americans in the military.

Why is it important to know that there were restrictions on African Americans during the war? Use text evidence to support your response.

_____

_____

_____

? **What do these passages suggest about the challenge the United States faced in World War II?**

Talk About It Reread the excerpts on pages 169 and 170. With a partner, talk about all the different groups that helped the United States win the war.

Cite Text Evidence Which groups helped contribute to the war effort and what conclusion can we draw by studying these groups?

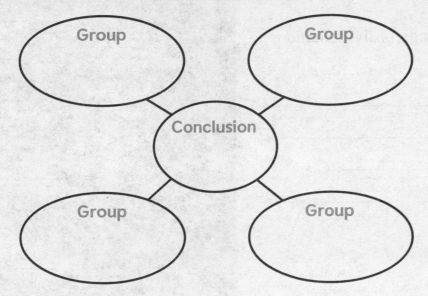

Write The contributions of different groups during the war were needed

because _____

_____

_____

_____

QUICK TIP
When I reread, I will pay close attention to the information that the author includes.

? How is the message of this World War II poster similar to the message of *The Unbreakable Code* and "Allies in Action"?

COLLABORATE

Talk About It Look at the poster and read the caption. Talk with a partner about what the men are doing.

Cite Text Evidence Underline clues in the poster that help you understand what the message is. Circle evidence in the caption that explains about the poster's purpose.

Write The message of this poster is similar to the message of the selections

because _____

_____

_____

_____

Library of Congress Prints and Photographs Division (LC-USZC2-5428)

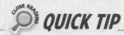

QUICK TIP

I see details in the poster that help me compare it to the selections I read this week.

Build for Your Navy! This poster was created by Robert Muchley between 1941 and 1942. It encourages skilled workmen to join the Navy during the war.

The Friend Who Changed My Life

Literature Anthology:
pages 450–461

? Why does the author include detailed descriptions of the narrator's, Theresa's, and Mary Lou's appearances and personalities?

Talk About It Reread pages 451–453. Turn to your partner and discuss what you know about the personalities of the characters in the story.

Cite Text Evidence What words and phrases does the author use to describe the characters? Write text evidence and explain the author's purpose.

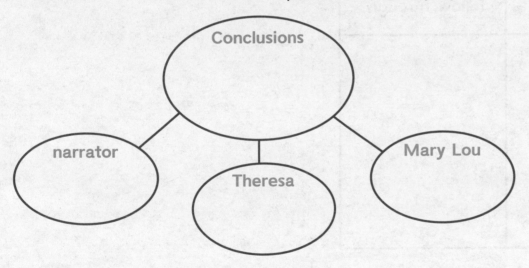

Conclusions

narrator

Theresa

Mary Lou

Write The author describes the personalities of the different girls because _____

_____

_____

_____

Tip of the Week

When I **reread**, I will think about why the author describes the characters. I look for text evidence for information about them.

Paco

Kali Nine LLC/iStock/360/Getty Images

? **Why does the author have Mary Lou threaten the narrator?**

COLLABORATE

Talk About It Reread the first column on page 454. Turn to your partner and talk about what you know about Mary Lou. Why do her words surprise you?

Cite Text Evidence Will Mary Lou actually hit the narrator? Cite text evidence to support your response.

Mary Lou's words and actions	Why Mary Lou's actions are surprising	Will Mary Lou follow through?

Write The author has Mary Lou threaten the narrator because _____

_____

_____

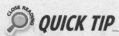
QUICK TIP

I can use these sentence frames when we talk about the characters in the story.

Mary Lou surprises the reader by . . .

The narrator needs to . . .

? How does the author use figurative language to show how the lives of the three girls have changed?

Talk About It Reread page 461. Turn to a partner and discuss how the image of falling dominos supports the author's organization of the story.

Cite Text Evidence How does the "domino effect" describe what happens to the narrator? Cite text evidence to support your response.

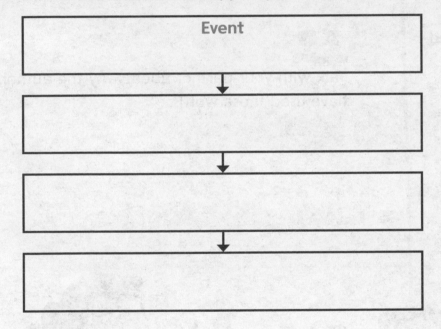

Event

Write Mary Lou's help has a "domino effect" on the narrator's life because _____

_____

_____

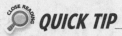

QUICK TIP

I can think about how a character's actions affect other characters.

Your Turn

Why is *The Friend Who Changed My Life* a meaningful and appropriate title for this story? Use these sentence frames to organize your text evidence.

The author helps me understand the characters by . . .

She organized the story to show me how . . .

This is important because it helps me understand that . . .

Go Digital!
Write your response online.

Choose Your Strategy: A Guide to Getting Along

1. *Tap. Tap. Tap.* Your classmate is tapping her foot on your desk and you are—tap, tap, tap—having a hard time concentrating. *What do you do?*

2. *Ha. Ha. Ha.* Your mismatched socks sent your friends into giggles, and the teasing hasn't stopped. Now your face is turning red and pink too. *What can you do?*

3. *Silence.* You and your best friend were chatting all morning, but at lunch, she is silent and decides to sit with another girl. *What will you do?*

4. *Snap.* You hear the sharp snap of a pencil behind you. Those two boys have started to pick on your classmate again. *What do you decide to do?*

Reread and use the prompts to take notes in the text.

Reread the excerpt. Circle the words the author uses to describe sounds. Describe the effect these words have on you.

_____

_____

COLLABORATE

Talk with your partner about why the author might have used those words.

Adjust Your Attitude

1.   One of the best ways to get along with others is to have a positive attitude. Remember, your attitude and your tone of voice affect those around you. If you respond to your classmate by yelling, it is likely that your classmate will react negatively, too, and this can escalate a minor problem to a major one. If you ask politely, you may get a better result.

2.   Finding a little humor in a situation can also make it less tense. So you are mortified by your mismatched socks, but stop and consider whether it is really worth getting angry. On second thought, it *is* funny. Sometimes laughter can be the best medicine, and a change of attitude can change your day.

Reread the excerpt. Circle the words that describe a difficult situation.

Then draw a box around how you could make the situation less tense.

COLLABORATE

With a partner, talk about how the author describes each situation and how they can be handled in new ways.

How does the author structure the text so that the reader understands the value of the advice he or she is offering?

_____

_____

_____

What is the author's purpose for writing this selection?

COLLABORATE

Talk About It Reread the excerpt on page 177. With a partner, discuss why the author would have written this text.

Cite Text Evidence How does the author use cause and effect relationships to help you solve a problem?

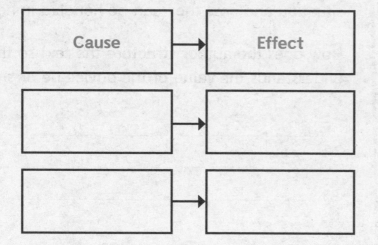

Cause	→	Effect
	→	
	→	

Write The author's purpose for writing this selection was _____

_____

_____

 **QUICK TIP**

When I reread, I will pay close attention to the details that the author provides.

? How do the authors of "A Fable," *The Friend Who Changed My Life,* and "Choose Your Strategy: A Guide to Getting Along" help you understand their lesson, or message?

Talk About It Read the fable. With a partner, discuss what the mice talk about doing.

Cite Text Evidence In the fable, circle words and phrases that describe what the mice want do to. Draw a box around the problem they face.

Write The authors help me understand each lesson by _____

_____

_____

_____

_____

_____

Akimasa Harada/Getty Images

QUICK TIP

I can use the authors' words to understand the lesson. I can compare a fable to text.

A Fable

Long ago, the mice met to decide how to outwit their enemy, the cat. A mouse got up and said, "You agree that our chief danger is in the sly manner in which the cat approaches. I propose that we get a bell and put it round the neck of the cat."

This met with applause, until an old mouse got up and said: "That is fine, but who is to bell the cat?"

Survival at 40 Below

? How does the author feel about the wood frog's adaptations to the cold?

Literature Anthology:
pages 468–483

COLLABORATE

Talk About It Reread page 471. Turn to your partner and discuss how the author talks about how frogs change in order to survive the Arctic.

Cite Text Evidence How does the author help you understand how she feels about how the frog adapts to the Arctic? Write text evidence.

Tip of the Week

When I **reread**, I can think about the words the author chooses to describe something. I look for text evidence to find her purpose.

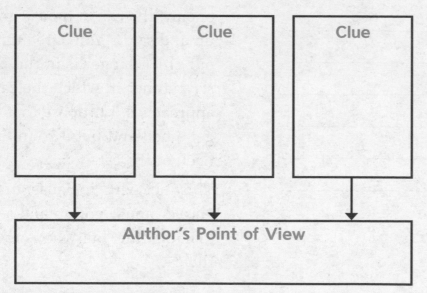

| Clue | Clue | Clue |

Author's Point of View

Ana

Write The author thinks that _____

_____

_____

Why does the author describe the arctic fox as an acrobat?

Talk About It Reread page 475. Turn to your partner and discuss how a fox is like an acrobat and how it is not.

Cite Text Evidence How are a fox and acrobat alike and different. Write text evidence in the diagram.

 **QUICK TIP**

I can use these sentence frames when we talk about text details.

The fox is similar to an acrobat because . . .

A fox is different because . . .

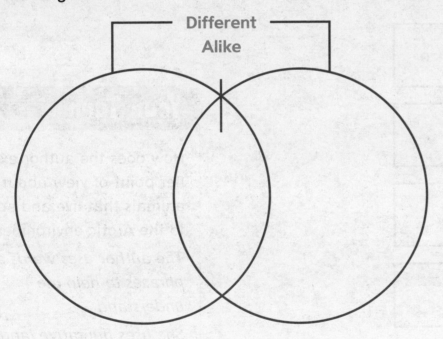

Different

Alike

Write The author describes the arctic fox as an acrobat _____

_____

? How does the author use sensory language to paint a picture with words on page 481?

Talk About It Reread page 481. Turn to a partner and talk about what the Arctic is like at the beginning of spring.

Cite Text Evidence What words and phrases help you picture what spring is like in the Arctic? Write text evidence.

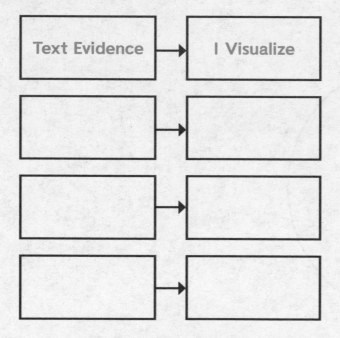

Text Evidence	I Visualize

Write The author uses sensory language to paint a picture _____

_____

_____

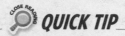

QUICK TIP

When I reread, I can think about how the author uses sensory words in descriptions.

Your Turn

How does the author express her point of view about the animals that live and adapt to the Arctic environment?

The author uses words and phrases to help me understand . . .

She uses figurative language to compare . . .

I know how she feels about animals because . . .

Go Digital!
Write your response online.

Why the Evergreen Trees Never Lose Their Leaves

1   "No, indeed," answered the birch-tree, drawing her fair leaves away. "We of the great forest have our own birds to help. I can do nothing for you."

2   "The birch is not very strong," said the little bird to itself, "and it might be that she could not hold me easily. I will ask the oak." So the bird said, "Great oak-tree, you are so strong, will you not let me live on your boughs till my friends come back in the springtime?"

3   "In the springtime!" cried the oak. "That is a long way off. How do I know what you might do in all that time? Birds are always looking for something to eat, and you might even eat up some of my acorns."

Reread and use the prompts to take notes in the text.

Reread the excerpt. Circle the lines of dialogue that tell you something about the trees' characters. Write what it reveals about the trees.

_____

_____

Talk with a partner about what the little bird's reaction to the birch-tree tells you about him. Underline the words in paragraph 2 that tell you his reaction.

1   "Come right here, then," said the friendly spruce-tree, for it was her voice that had called. "You shall live on my warmest branch all winter if you choose."

2   "Will you really let me?" asked the little bird eagerly.

3   "Indeed, I will," answered the kind-hearted spruce-tree. "If your friends have flown away, it is time for the trees to help you. Here is the branch where my leaves are thickest and softest."

4   "My branches are not very thick," said the friendly pine-tree, "but I am big and strong, and I can keep the north wind from you and the spruce."

5   "I can help too," said a little juniper-tree. "I can give you berries all winter long, and every bird knows that juniper berries are good."

Reread the excerpt. Underline the sentence in paragraph 1 that tells what the spruce-tree offers the little bird.

Underline the sentence in paragraph 5 that tells what the juniper-tree offers the little bird.

COLLABORATE

Talk about the trees with a partner. How do they respond to the bird? Circle words that show what the trees are like.

What do these trees do? Use text evidence to support your response.

_____

_____

Why does the author contrast the behavior of the two groups of trees?

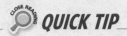 **QUICK TIP**

When I reread, I can pay close attention to the consequences of the characters' actions.

COLLABORATE

Talk About It Reread the excerpts on pages 183 and 184. With a partner, discuss the different groups of trees. How are they different?

Cite Text Evidence What words and phrases describe the behavior of the two groups of trees? Write what it tells you about the trees.

Text Evidence	→	What It Tells
	→	
	→	
	→	
	→	

Write The author shows the two groups of trees differently because _____

_____

_____

_____

? **How are the adaptations you see in this photograph similar to the adaptations described in *Survival at 40 Below* and "Why the Evergreen Trees Never Lose Their Leaves"?**

COLLABORATE

Talk About It Look at the photograph and read the caption. With a partner, talk about what you see and how this animal has adapted to its habitat.

Cite Text Evidence Draw a box around details that help show the setting of the photograph. Circle the hare's adaptations. Underline evidence in the caption that tells more about how this animal adapts. Think about how these adaptations help the hare survive.

Write The adaptations in this photograph are similar to the ones in the selections because _____

_____

_____

_____

_____

_____

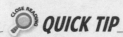
QUICK TIP
I see clues in this photograph that show how this animal survives in the winter. I can compare it to the selections I read this week.

imgr2003/iStock/Getty Images Plus/Getty Images

Can you see this snowshoe hare? His fur turns white in winter. During summer months, this animal is brown. It takes 10 weeks for its fur to change completely.

Planting the Trees of Kenya

? How do the details about Wangari's education foreshadow her efforts to improve Kenya?

Literature Anthology: pages 490–501

Talk About It Reread pages 492–493. Turn to your partner and talk about how Wangari feels about Kenya's beauty and what she learns at college.

Cite Text Evidence What clues in the text and illustration help you see how the author is foreshadowing what Wangari will do? Write text evidence.

Illustration Clues	Text Evidence	What This Foreshadows

Write The author foreshadows what Wangari will do by _____

_____

Tip of the Week

When I **reread**, I can think about how the author's descriptions give me clues to the story's meaning.

Yasmine

How do the events following Wangari's return to Kenya build on an idea introduced at the beginning of the story?

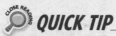 **QUICK TIP**

I can use these sentence frames when we talk about the trees.

During Wangari's childhood, trees are...

After Wangari returns to Kenya, trees are...

COLLABORATE

Talk About It Reread page 495. Turn to your partner and talk about what Wangari saw when she returned to Kenya.

Cite Text Evidence What words and phrases show what Wangari saw when she returned? Write how that builds on what she knew as a child.

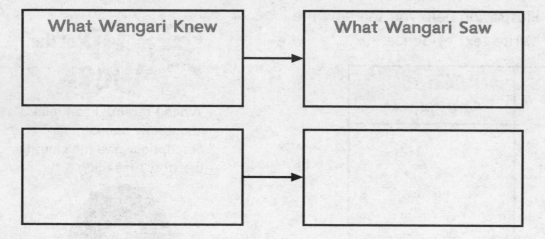

What Wangari Knew	What Wangari Saw

Write What Wangari finds when she returns _____

_____

_____

? How does the author's use of figurative language help you understand how Wangari helped the people tend to the trees?

COLLABORATE

Talk About It Reread page 501. Turn to a partner and talk about how the author compares the soil to people.

Cite Text Evidence What words and phrases show how the author uses personification when talking about the soil? Write text evidence.

Text Evidence	What it Suggests	Effect

Write The author's use of figurative language _____

_____

_____

QUICK TIP
When I reread, I can see how the author uses personification to help me understand the story.

Your Turn

How does the way the author uses language show how Wangari helped the land and the people of Kenya?

In the beginning, the author introduces the ideas . . .

The author develops these ideas by . . .

The author uses figurative language to . . .

This is important because I can see how . . .

Go Digital!
Write your response online.

The Park Project

1   Two third-grade students, Adeline Dixon and Sophia Kimbell, saw that Letty Walter Park, a park in their Indiana community, was in poor condition and needed repairs. The students wanted to plant new trees along the park's creek, but that project required money, which the students did not have. So they decided to write a letter asking a community organization for money to restore the park.

2   "We wrote it by ourselves," Sophia said. "Our parents spell-checked, but that was it."

3   Happily, the money was granted. The two students and their classmates bought and planted trees along the park's creek. One tree was named The Survivor Tree because it had grown from a seed taken from a tree that survived the Oklahoma City bombing in 1995.

Reread and use the prompts to take notes in the text.

In paragraph 1, circle the problems the girls saw at the park. Underline the sentence that explains what the girls did to get their project off the ground. Write it here:

_____

_____

_____

Reread paragraph 3. Talk with a partner about what happened after the money was granted. What was special about one of the trees? Draw a box around the text evidence that supports your answer.

[4] Unfortunately, the park improvements did not last long. Later that year, powerful storms caused by a nearby hurricane destroyed most of the trees the students had planted. Only two trees remained standing, including The Survivor Tree. The third graders were saddened by the destruction, but they held on to their dream of improving the park.

[5] Two years later, Adeline and Sophia, now fifth graders, wrote another letter to the same community organization. Again they urged the group to donate money so students could fix up Letty Walter Park. Again money was granted for planting trees and for further improvements, such as adding two park benches and spreading mulch—a mix of leaves and straw—on the playground.

Reread paragraph 4. Circle clues that show what happened to the park improvements. Underline how the third graders felt.

COLLABORATE

Reread paragraph 5. With a partner, talk about what Adeline and Sophia did two years later. Make marks in the margin beside text evidence that shows what the girls did. Write it here:

_____

_____

_____

_____

? **Why does the author continue the story into Adeline and Sophia's fifth-grade year?**

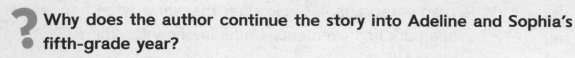
COLLABORATE

Talk About It Reread the excerpts on pages 190 and 191. With a partner, talk about what happens after the students plant trees the first time.

Cite Text Evidence In the chart below, write what happened first, what happened after that, and how the students responded.

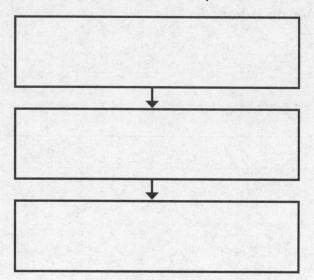

Write This sequence reveals that the author's purpose for writing the story is ___

_____

_____

_____

_____

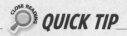
QUICK TIP

When I reread, I will think about story events to help me understand the author's purpose.

? How is the way the artist shows people impacting their world similar to the way the authors show it in *Planting the Trees of Kenya* and "The Park Project"?

ImageZoo/SuperStock

COLLABORATE

Talk About It Look at the illustration. Read the caption. Talk with a partner about what you see. Choose some images and talk about how their actions impact their community.

Cite Text Evidence Draw a box around details in the picture that show how the people make an impact. Circle how you know how they feel about what they are doing.

Write The artist and authors show people's impact on their world

by _____

_____

_____

_____

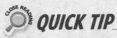

QUICK TIP

I see people making an impact. This will help me compare the illustration to the selections I read this week.

This illustration shows eight people participating in a tree planting activity in an urban garden.

You Are My Music

? How does the poet use words and phrases to describe what Ana means to her sister, Aida?

Literature Anthology: pages 506–508

COLLABORATE

Talk About It Reread the first and last stanzas on pages 506 and 507. Talk with a partner about how Aida describes Ana.

Cite Text Evidence What details in the poem help you understand the connection between Ana's hands and her sister? Write text evidence.

Text Evidence	What It Tells About Ana

CLOSE READING

Tip of the Week

When I **reread**, I will think about how the author uses figurative language.

Frank

Write Aida describes Ana's hands _____

_____

_____

Toby Burrows/Photodisc/Getty Images

You and I

How does the poet use figurative language to help you understand her message?

Talk About It Reread the second stanza on page 508. Turn to your partner and talk about what "splits us each in two" means.

Cite Text Evidence What phrases help you understand the poet's message? Write text evidence and tell the message.

Text Evidence	Message

Write The poet helps me see the message _____

_____

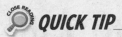

QUICK TIP

I can think about how the author uses figurative language in a poem.

Your Turn

Think about the figurative language in the poems. How do the poets use it to communicate a message about people and the connections they make?

The metaphors in the first poem . . .

The figurative language in the second poem . . .

These techniques show that people can connect with each other by . . .

Go Digital!
Write your response online.

A Time to Talk

? Why are the first two lines of the poem important to the poem's meaning?

Talk About It Reread the poem on page 510. Turn to your partner and discuss what the poet is saying in the first two lines.

Cite Text Evidence What clues help you understand how the first two lines affect the rest of the poem? Write text evidence and explain how.

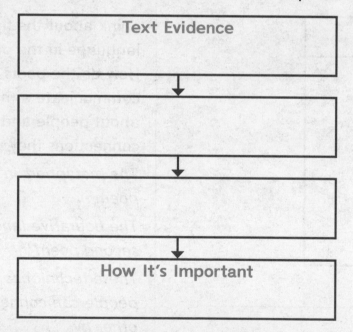

Text Evidence

How It's Important

Write The first two lines affect the rest of the poem because _____

_____

_____

QUICK TIP

When I reread, I will think about how the opening of a poem can set up the rest of it.

? **What do you learn about the narrator from this poem?**

COLLABORATE

Talk About It Reread the poem on page 510. With a partner, talk about what choice the narrator of the poem has to make.

Cite Text Evidence What words and phrases describe what kind of person the narrator is. Write text evidence in the web.

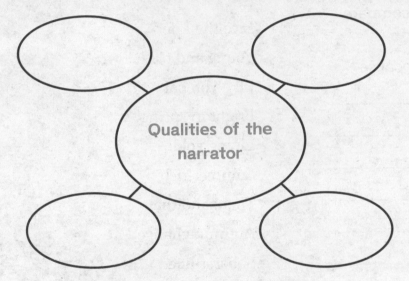

Qualities of the narrator

Write The narrator of this poem _____

_____

_____

_____

QUICK TIP

Memorize and recite the poem, "A Time to Talk." This will help you understand the narrator better.

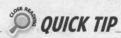

QUICK TIP

I see what the poet feels is important. This will help me compare the poems I read.

? How are the connections made by Alfred, Lord Tennyson similar to the connections made by the poets of "You Are My Music" and "A Time to Talk"?

COLLABORATE

Talk About It Read the poem. Talk with a partner about what the oak tree symbolizes in the poem.

Cite Text Evidence Circle words in the poem that help you visualize an oak tree. Underline words and phrases that compare the oak tree to a person.

Write The connections made by the poets are similar because

_____

_____

_____

_____

_____

_____

The Oak

Live thy Life,

Young and old,

Like yon oak,

Bright in spring,

Living gold;

Summer-rich

Then; and then

Autumn-changed

Soberer-hued

Gold again.

All his leaves

Fall'n at length,

Look, he stands,

Trunk and bough

Naked strength.

— Alfred, Lord Tennyson

Kevin Britland/Alamy